Cyberdiplomacy

I dedicate this book to Jenny. Everything good or worthwhile in my life I owe her.

Cyberdiplomacy

Managing Security and Governance Online

Shaun Riordan

polity

First published in 2019 by Polity Press

Polity Press
65 Bridge Street
Cambridge CB2 1UR, UK

Polity Press
101 Station Landing
Suite 300
Medford, MA 02155, USA

ISBN-13: 978-1-5095-3407-4
ISBN-13: 978-1-5095-3408-1 (pb)

A catalogue record for this book is available from the British Library.

Library of Congress Cataloging-in-Publication Data

Names: Riordan, Shaun, author.
Title: Cyberdiplomacy : managing security and governance online / Shaun Riordan.
Description: Cambridge, UK ; Medford, MA : Polity Press, 2019. | Includes bibliographical references and index.
Identifiers: LCCN 2018037565 (print) | LCCN 2018040824 (ebook) | ISBN 9781509534098 (Epub) | ISBN 9781509534074 (hardback) | ISBN 9781509534081 (pbk.)
Subjects: LCSH: Internet governance. | Cyberspace. | Diplomacy.
Classification: LCC TK5105.8854 (ebook) | LCC TK5105.8854 .R56 2019 (print) | DDC 353.1/3028558–dc23
LC record available at https://lccn.loc.gov/2018037565

Typeset in 11 on 13 pt Sabon by Toppan Best-set Premedia Limited
Printed and bound in the United Kingdom by Clays Ltd, Elcograf S.p.A.

For further information on Polity, visit our website: politybooks.com

Contents

Preface

I recently took part in a panel about the future relationship between diplomacy and science. A fellow panellist bemoaned the difficulties of achieving international agreement about how to govern the internet. He complained that the different actors had different motivations, different objectives and different ideologies; they even spoke different languages. I couldn't help replying: 'welcome to the world of the diplomat.' If all countries shared the same views on global governance in physical space, then we would not need diplomats. The same is true of cyberspace.

When the internet began, many argued that it would revolutionise international relations. In cyberspace there would be no borders. The power and influence of the Westphalian nation-state would be fatally undermined. Traditional diplomats and diplomacy would no longer be needed. Citizen ambassadors would talk directly unto citizen ambassadors. The internet has undoubtedly changed the context in which international relations play out. New governmental and non-governmental actors have been empowered by the new information communication technologies as they join the debates about new international security agendas. And yet the nation-state is still with us and recently has even grown in relevance. Far from being a flat, borderless realm, cyberspace has become another domain for geopolitical conflict, as well as debates and disagreements over international governance. Where there are geopolitical conflicts and disagreements over international governance, there ought to be diplomats and diplomacy. But oddly they are noticeable mainly by their absence.

There are three vectors in diplomacy: agency (who is the diplomat), process (the tools and techniques of diplomacy) and subject matter (the area to which diplomacy is applied). So far, in relation to the new technologies, the focus of both scholars and practitioners has been on process: the implications of digital tools for diplomats and how diplomats can use these to advance broader diplomatic agendas. There has been some good work on how digital tools can support consular work. But this is counterbalanced by an obsession with the use of social media to advance public diplomacy agendas. Ambassadors blog, first secretaries tweet, and third secretaries have pages on Facebook. Insufficient thought has been given to the implications of using social media platforms and search engines designed to monetise data to promote international debate. Only slowly is it dawning that social media platforms facilitate information warfare and frustrate public diplomacy. The very algorithms that ensure efficient monetisation of data weaponise information. They ensure that the fake news of information warfare reaches the echo chambers predisposed to believe it while limiting the reach of public diplomacy to those who are already in agreement. Diplomats and scholars need to raise their game.

This book focuses on agency and subject matter. It explores what it means to be a diplomat and, in particular, whether there is a diplomatic approach or way of dealing with the world. It then examines how such a diplomatic approach can be applied to the various problems arising in cyberspace, whether related to internet governance or the various forms of conflict arising from illicit penetration of foreign computer systems. So far we seem to believe that both kinds of problem can be resolved with technological solutions. The techies built the internet, so the techies can sort out the problems. This is profoundly mistaken. This would be the equivalent to leaving all international problems in physical space to the military. The military, like the techies in cyberspace, have their role, but stability is likely to be enhanced by having the diplomats along too. To put it another way, technical solutions are necessary but not sufficient.

My colleague on the panel on diplomacy and science was concerned about the debates on internet governance. There is a struggle for the soul of the internet between those who advocate the original vision of a free internet and those who support the idea of establishing government control under the jurisdiction of international governmental organisations. The negotiating skills of the diplomat will be needed to edge towards a compromise. On the same panel, we discussed the problems in distinguishing between different types of computer penetration. For example, penetration designed to gather information and monitor developments looks very like penetration in preparation for a future attack on critical infrastructure. How do you distinguish between cyberespionage and preparations for cyberwar? Being unable to do so increases the risks of conflict escalation, including in the physical world. Our conclusion was that there is a need for a better understanding of the motivations and intentions of the other side. Recent evidence suggests that humans are remarkably good at identifying intentions, providing they enjoy prolonged and repeated face-to-face contact. Repeated face-to-face contact with foreign politicians and officials – who on earth would do that? The cyberspace that was once thought to make diplomats and diplomacy irrelevant may instead be making them more important by the day, and they are carrying out very traditional-looking functions. Time for diplomats to stop messing with social media and get back to the serious stuff.

This book has arisen from conversations with a broad range of colleagues from across the diplomatic studies and international relations spectrum. Appropriately, many of these exchanges have been through Twitter (which is better for academic exchanges than diplomacy!), while others have been at workshops, especially those organised by Corneliu Bjola, Ilan Manor and Jennifer Cassidy at the Digital Diplomacy Project in Oxford. I have also benefited from participating in webinars with Jovan Kurbalija and Katharina Höne at the DiploFoundation in Geneva. Mikkel Larsen's wonderful #Digital Diplomacy podcast was another opportunity to bounce ideas around. My thinking on diplomacy in general has been developed through conversations over the years with Paul Sharp, Jan Melissen, Brian Hocking, Pedro Baños and Velina Tchakarova. In Madrid, Colonel Ángel Gómez de Ágreda, formerly of the Spanish Cyber Command, read the entire manuscript and made detailed suggestions. My editors at Polity, Louise Knight and Nekane Tanaka Galdos, were endlessly patient and encouraging, and the anonymous reviewers offered constructive criticism. I am grateful to them all, with the caveat that any errors or misjudgements are mine alone. My mother and my sons Tom, Fergus and Rory encouraged (bullied!) me to finish the book, which is dedicated to my wife Jenny.

1

Introduction

The Threat

In January 2018 the British minister of defence, Gavin Williamson, warned that a Russian cyberattack against the UK's critical infrastructure could leave thousands dead.[1] This may have been a bid to increase the defence budget, yet in May 2017 the Wannacry ransomware attack caused chaos in Britain's hospitals, as well as hitting corporate giants such as FedEx and the Spanish telecommunications giant Telefonica. The aim was criminal, freezing computers and then unfreezing them in return for a ransom payment in the digital currency Bitcoin, but it demonstrated the vulnerability of critical infrastructure.[2] Cyberattacks against governments and companies appear to be continual, whether to steal data (including intellectual property) or money or in preparation for future attacks. Most are never reported in public, either because governments do not want to reveal sensitive information or because companies want to protect their reputations and share price. But enough does enter the public domain to reveal a digital space parallel to the physical space, where digital equipment and information interact, and where bad things are happening. The effect of these bad things is not limited to this digital space but can impact on the physical space. For example, when the Wannacry virus hit computers in British hospitals, blocking access to key data, operations had to be suspended and emergency units closed down. This put at risk the security and welfare of thousands of patients, even if this was not the initial intention of the hackers who had launched the ransomware attack.

So far, attacks against computers and other digital systems designed to cause real damage in the physical world (what the military refer to as 'kinetic effects') have been rare. The best known is the Stuxnet campaign against the Iranian nuclear enrichment facilities, especially the facility at Natanz. This allegedly joint US–Israeli operation, code-named Olympic Games, targeted the centrifuges essential to the enrichment of uranium, exaggerating their speeds until they broke.[3] It is possible that the United States has also launched cyberattacks against North Korea's ballistic missile programme, provoking failures in missile tests.[4] But, even if the number of cyberattacks with kinetic effects is so far small, the number of broader cyberattacks, and the range of state and non-state actors developing the capacity to launch them, is growing. These cyberattacks can be broadly categorised as cyberwar, cyberterrorism, cyberespionage and cybercrime. In cyberwar, state actors penetrate foreign computer systems with the aim of damaging the systems themselves, using them to create kinetic effects in the physical world or to prepare the ground to launch attacks in the future. In cyberterrorism, non-state groups penetrate computer systems with the intention of damaging the systems or using them to create kinetic effects. Interestingly, we have not yet seen genuine cyberterrorism. Terrorist groups such as Islamic State have undoubtedly recruited internet engineers, but their online activities have so far been limited to cybercrime (bank raids to raise funds) or online information warfare (see below). In cyberespionage, state and non-state actors penetrate systems to steal information (including personal data, data about capabilities and intentions, and intellectual property). In cybercrime, non-state actors (criminals) penetrate computer systems to generate financial income illegally. This might include straightforward theft (the Russian GameOver criminal network simply drained $6.9 million in a single attack) but also the stealing of information to blackmail companies or using ransomware (the same GameOver network is thought to have made over $1 million from ransomware attacks). These distinctions are not watertight. Governments may work with criminals, piggy-backing criminal attacks for cyberwar or cyberespionage purposes.

Apart from attacking computer systems, state actors can use social media and other digital tools to spread information and propaganda. Russia has been accused of using social media such as Facebook and Twitter to influence elections in the US and France and the Brexit referendum in the UK.[5] Extremist groups use social media to increase social tensions, spread hate messages and recruit members. Concern is growing in the West about the use of social media to spread misleading or distorted information, or sometimes plain lies, increasingly referred to as 'fake news'. Talk has begun of cyber information warfare.[6] The EU has created a strategic communication task force (the EU East StratCom Task Force) to counter what it sees as misinformation being spread by state-backed Russian media. Sometimes the use of social media is combined with penetration attacks. During the 2016 US presidential election campaign, Russian hackers penetrated the computer systems of the Democratic National Committee, in particular the emails of John Podesta, which were then released through WikiLeaks. It is not clear what impact they had on the election result, but they did portray a Democratic candidate out of touch with the concerns of ordinary voters.

Cyberspace is a controversial term, with many different definitions. However, it captures the idea of a space parallel to physical space but closely interrelated with it, where digital information and equipment interact. As we have seen, what happens in cyberspace can impact on what happens in physical space. But what happens in physical space also impacts on cyberspace. In as far as cyberspace consists of digital information and equipment designed and built by humans, it is a man-made creation. Its shape and functioning are defined by human decisions, whether state or non-state actors. It grows with every new piece of digital equipment and application. The developing Internet of Things, where everyday household items, cars, and other machinery and equipment are connected to the internet, represents another significant expansion of cyberspace. Putting 'things' online in this way increases not only convenience and productivity but also vulnerabilities, both of individuals and of the system. The introduction of fifth-generation mobile telephony (5G) will represent another increase in connectivity and in the scope of cyberspace. But, as a man-made creation, cyberspace needs man-made rules to govern it. Internet governance may not seem as exciting as the cybersecurity issues outlined above, but it is crucial to how the internet and global society will develop in the twenty-first century. How the internet is governed will shape how, and in whose interests, cyberspace operates. The key issues reflect debates in physical space. Who manages the physical structure of the internet? How are online service providers to be regulated, and where do they pay their taxes? Shall the internet be global or national? What is the balance between freedom of expression and the control of extremism and hate speech? How can we protect privacy and individuals' data, and what are the prices we are willing to pay in economic efficiency and security? How to combat fake news and manipulation of social media? At the core of these debates is a more general point that has nothing to do directly with cyberspace. How can we agree new international rules in a multipolar world where the old Western consensus on international norms and institutions has broken down, and where non-state as well as state actors play an increasingly important role?[7]

Cyberdiplomacy vs Digital Diplomacy

Diplomats have always been behind the curve in cyberspace. Concerns about security, and the obsession with secrecy, made them reluctant to use computers, let alone link up to the internet (the massive release to WikiLeaks of US diplomatic cables suggests that their fears may not have been misplaced). Most foreign ministries did not use emails until the turn of millennium. Since then a plethora of terms has entered the vocabulary as diplomats and scholars of diplomacy have played desperate catch-up. Most prominent have been digital diplomacy, cyberdiplomacy and e-diplomacy. These have often been used interchangeably, causing not a little confusion in the process. Some time ago I suggested distinguishing between digital diplomacy and cyberdiplomacy.[8] I suggested that digital diplomacy should refer to the use of digital tools to pursue wider diplomatic objectives, and that cyberdiplomacy should refer to the use of diplomatic tools and mindsets in resolving, or at least managing, the problems in cyberspace. Thus digital diplomacy is the application of digital tools to diplomacy, whereas cyberdiplomacy is the application of diplomacy to cyberspace. Gradually this distinction seems to be catching on (with the term e-diplomacy slipping from common usage). These are the definitions I will use here.

This book will focus on cyberdiplomacy. It aims to explore how a diplomatic approach can help resolve or manage the cybersecurity, online information warfare and internet governance problems identified above. Much has been written about digital diplomacy, whether in books, academic journals or more popular blogs.[9] The nature and importance of digital diplomacy has been, appropriately, much debated through social media. However, very little has been written about cyberdiplomacy (a paper written by André Barrinha and Thomas Renard in *Global Affairs* sets out the key challenges).[10] In part this reflects a prejudice that sees cyberspace as so different and separate from physical space that only technical solutions apply. If cyberspace is where digital equipment interacts with digital solutions, then digital solutions must be found for the problems that arise there. But in this book I will argue that, as cyberspace is as much a human creation as physical space (in many respects more so), non-technical approaches must accompany technical solutions. Relying only on technical solutions to resolve the governance, security, criminal and espionage issues arising in cyberspace is equivalent to relying only on military solutions in physical space. Cyberdiplomacy must complement technical measures in cyberspace just as diplomacy complements military measures in physical space.

This book will not ignore digital diplomacy completely. Digital diplomacy will feature through offering digital tools which cyberdiplomacy can deploy in pursuing its broader objectives. In this sense, as in many others, cyberdiplomacy is little different from ordinary diplomacy. It is distinguished primarily by being applied to cyberspace rather than the physical space. A theme that will be explored in this book is how much difference that really makes and the extent to which cyberdiplomacy should be integrated within broader diplomacy. Digital diplomacy will also feature through the problems associated with it, or which it provokes, and which may require the help of cyberdiplomacy to manage. The extent to which digital tools are used in public diplomacy to counter information warfare risks escalation to an online free for all which might require cyberdiplomacy to de-escalate. Alternatively, cyberdiplomacy may be deployed to negotiate new norms to restrain online behaviour by state and non-state actors, helping to manage the problem without escalation. Digital diplomacy will also be affected by many of the issues on the internet governance agenda. For example, the debates on data protection at national and international level may limit the use foreign ministries can make of Big Data, whether in intelligence gathering and analysis or in providing targeted consular protection and support for distressed citizens abroad.

Digital Diplomacy

Digital diplomacy has compounded its own problems through an excessive focus on social media as a means to influence and assess foreign public opinion, a dependence which has led both to an online presence being seen as an end in itself and to less attention being paid to other, possibly more useful, digital tools. The disconnect between digital diplomacy and broader diplomatic strategies has been particularly limiting, with many diplomats having no clear idea why they are using particular social media.[11] Many fail to understand the distinctions between different platforms, with Twitter more effective for immediate comment and reaction and Facebook and LinkedIn for more thoughtful attempts to influence opinion. Twitter poses particular problems for diplomats. It requires very short reaction times, with comments or replies to tweets having to be almost immediate to be relevant or have impact. There is no time for a diplomat in an embassy to consult with her foreign ministry before responding. Being effective on Twitter, as opposed to just using it as a means for publishing pithy press releases (which is what most foreign ministries do), requires delegating the authority to the diplomat in the field to tweet and retweet without reference to his ministry, or even his ambassador. Few foreign ministries have shown themselves willing to do this.

Social media such as Facebook and search engines such as Google pose their own problems for diplomats. The algorithms which drive them are designed to maximise marketing revenues by shaping what you receive to what can be deduced about your tastes and interests. This means that adverts on Facebook will be for products you are most likely to buy. But this also means that the friend proposals and the news you receive will also be filtered towards your known opinions and tastes. As we will discuss later, this reinforces the tendency towards echo chambers, where we socialise online only with people like ourselves and only listen to news and opinions which reinforce our existing prejudices. On the one hand, this is taken advantage of by state and non-state actors using social media to spread misinformation and fragment foreign societies. On the other hand, it limits diplomats depending on social media to speaking only to those who already agree with them. While reinforcing the support among like-minded supporters is no doubt useful, public diplomacy should surely seek to reach out to those who disagree as well. Dependence on social media for public diplomacy makes this difficult to achieve. The problem is compounded by the algorithms behind search engines, which condition and prioritise the search results produced. In 2016, far-right groups gamed Google's algorithm so that a search for 'Did the Holocaust happen?' produced a series of Holocaust denial sites. A major task for cyberdiplomacy may be convincing social media platforms to share more details of their algorithms.[12]

Whether or not a tweet or a post has an impact or not is largely a question of luck. The vast majority of tweets and posts are not 'liked', retweeted or shared even once. Even if a social media campaign appears to be successful ('goes viral') it may not achieve its objectives; it may even prove counterproductive. On the night of 14–15 April 2014, 276 schoolgirls were kidnapped from the Nigerian village of Chibok by the Islamist terrorist group Boko Haram. An online campaign was launched to secure their return with the hashtag #BringBackOurGirls. The campaign quickly went viral. Michelle Obama retweeted from the Oval Office of the White House. In terms of a social media campaign it was successful, but it did nothing to secure the release of the girls (some have escaped or been rescued, but not because of the social media campaign). On the other hand, it did significantly raise the profile of Boko Haram, which previously had been a relatively obscure and unknown terrorist group. A social media campaign which sought the release of the kidnapped girls ended up benefiting only the terrorists who had kidnapped them. Given the difficulties and problems of social media as diplomatic tools, this book will focus on other digital tools that can support cyber (and non-cyber) diplomacy. These include online platforms for scenario-building and simulation exercises, gamification (the use of computer games for promoting learning and influencing debate) and the potential of blockchains for supporting bottom-up global governance.

Cyberspace and Physical Space

An underlying argument of this book is that cyberspace and physical space are not as different as some experts maintain – a crucial argument if we are to contend that diplomacy is as relevant to cyberspace as it is to physical space. As the argument is explored, it will also become apparent to what extent diplomacy in cyberspace is different from diplomacy in physical space. As the two spaces integrate, this may not be as much as one might first suppose. Interestingly, the developments in cyberspace in many ways mirror those in physical space, suggesting that, although diplomacy may be different in the twenty-first century, it may be different in strikingly similar ways in the two spaces. The digital technologies which have facilitated the participation of non-state actors in international debates in physical space equally facilitate their participation in cyberspace debates. Such non-state actors include companies, NGOs, user groups, academics and the media (new and old). Even individuals, converted into star bloggers or YouTube stars, can now have serious impact on key debates, and must be engaged with and taken serious by diplomats, whether tackling issues in cyberspace or physical space. Both cyberspace and physical space also have their darker non-state actors. Extremists and terrorists prowl physical space, launching attacks and threatening the security of the citizen. But they also prowl cyberspace, where they are joined by factories of trolls in Russia and patriot hackers in China. Organised crime exists in both physical and cyberspace. The darker non-state elements in cyberspace often have ambiguous relations with their governments, making attribution for cyberattacks difficult. In addition, non-state governments at all levels, from regional groupings such as the EU, NATO or the Shanghai Cooperation Organisation down to city governments and town halls, are active in both physical and cyberspace. The decision by President Trump to withdraw the United States from the Paris Accord on climate change may have reinforced this tendency towards subnational or paradiplomacy. Outraged state and city governments in the US have affirmed their intention to remain in the process, meaning that at least some of the climate change debate will have to be prosecuted at their level. Cities and other subnational governments may find similar interest in bypassing national governments to engage with issues such as internet governance and cybersecurity. In short, diplomats, whether dealing with physical or cyberspace, will have to deal with multiple state and non-state actors operating in multilevel and heterogeneous networks.

The duality between the cybersecurity and internet governance agendas parallels the conflict in physical space between the global issues (or new international security) and geopolitical agendas in physical space. The global issues or new international security agenda emerged around the turn of the twenty-first century as international security began to be seen less in terms of the security or stability of the state and more in terms of the security and economic well-being of the individual within the state. This was initially driven by the need to include international terrorism within the international security agenda, especially after the 9/11 attacks. But the focus on the security and economic welfare of the individual resulted in the agenda being expanded to incorporate issues such as pandemic disease, environmental degradation, poverty, migration, financial stability, climate change and organised crime. The issues on this agenda share several features: they tend to be existential for the survival of mankind rather than the security of any state – in other words, they threaten all states; they tend to be interrelated and interdependent, so that it is difficult to tackle them individually; they require global cooperation and collaboration – no single state or group of states can tackle them on their own; and they require collaboration that goes beyond national governments, to embrace a wide range of state and non-state actors. In the early years of the twenty-first century, it looked as if this would be the prominent agenda in international relations.[13] European diplomacy was largely reconfigured to deal, almost exclusively, with this agenda. However, since about 2005 we have seen a gradual return of more traditional geopolitical agendas focused on the projection and balance of power, zones of influence, and control of territory and resources. Russia has invaded Georgia and Crimea and destabilised Eastern Ukraine. China has developed the One Belt, One Road strategy to project its power globally while building up its military forces (and constructing artificial islands on disputed reefs) in the South China Sea. Saudi Arabia and Iran are locked in a proxy war for hegemony in the Middle East. This return of geopolitics threatens to undermine progress on the global issues or new international security agenda, as states are forced to prioritise short-term geopolitical threats over the longer-term global threats. Similarly, cybersecurity conflicts undermine the prospects of making progress on the internet governance agenda, while at the same time threatening to take over the agenda. The existence and growth of cyberspace may also promote geopolitical or great power conflict in physical space by appearing to offer low-risk, and more deniable, means of attacking or undermining a rival. Twenty-first-century diplomacy will have to deal with both types of agenda in both physical space and cyberspace, understanding the relationships and interdependencies between them.

Finally, both physical and cyberspace must confront the fragmentation of the global rule sets that, until recently, governed international political and economic relations. These rule sets were essentially derived from the contingencies of European history and imposed by US hegemony. As US global hegemony has declined, following the Iraq War and the economic crisis, these rule sets and the value systems underlying them are increasingly being questioned by emerging non-European powers.[14] As the global consensus on how the world should be regulated breaks down, it becomes increasingly difficult to create new international institutions or agree new rule sets. Rising powers move to set up alternative or rival institutions. New models may have to be developed for new areas of global governance and regulation, building from the bottom up rather than the top down and engaging the multiple state and non-state actors who have a stake in the outcome. This will be as true of the physical world as of cyberspace.

The core argument of this book is that diplomacy must complement security and technical measures if cyberspace is not to decline into a Hobbesian world of perpetual war of all against all. In one sense the Hobbesian cyberspace has already arrived, with a growing number of cyber-actors, state and non-state, constantly penetrating computer systems in pursuit of information or money or to damage or prepare for damage in the future. Without some corrective action, cyber escalation and proliferation will continue. As we will see later, the Stuxnet attack on Iran's nuclear centrifuges provoked Iran to develop a cyber capability which it then deployed against Saudi Arabia. As long as we depend on technical and security measures, the escalation and proliferation will continue. The same is true of cyber information warfare, where the temptation to respond to attempts to destabilise Western societies in kind risks the weaponisation of social media and increasing instability and social fragmentation in physical space. The argument therefore is that there is a diplomatic approach to cyberspace – what I call cyberdiplomacy – which can help claw cyberspace back from Hobbes and develop a rudimentary corpus of norms and rules of the game that introduce some stability and predictability. In a sense this becomes the equivalent of international law in physical space: not perfect, but with just sufficient incentive to keep barbarity at bay. A secondary argument will be, as suggested above, that the diplomacy, and diplomats, skills and mindsets, needed for cyberspace will be essentially the same as what is needed for dealing with the physical space in the twenty-first century, and that foreign ministries should engage with them simultaneously, not regarding them as two radically different worlds.

A Diplomatic Approach?

The argument that there is a diplomatic approach to cyberspace begs the question of what a diplomatic approach is. Is there something that is diplomacy? Or, more relevantly, is there a way of thinking and behaving that is diplomatic? Is there a series of criteria that allows us to decide if an actor is behaving in a diplomatic way or if an approach is diplomatic as opposed to alternative means (such as lobbying, NGO campaigning)? The question has arisen in diplomatic studies because of the desire to talk about non-state actors in a variety of new diplomacies (e.g., sports diplomacy, business diplomacy and, indeed, cyberdiplomacy). The question sounds abstract and abstruse, but it is central. If there is a diplomatic approach to the problems of cyberspace, it must be spelled out. It must also be explained if this diplomatic approach is limited to government diplomats (there are many who argue that diplomacy is limited to those covered by the Vienna Convention on Diplomatic

Relations) or whether non-state actors can also be said to be acting as cyber (or any other kind of) diplomats. If there is a clear sense of what it means for a non-state actor to behave in a diplomat-like way, a further question is how such individuals deal with those actors, state or non-state, who do not. This book will therefore start by explaining what it means to be a diplomat and by attempting to sketch out a diplomat-like way of approaching cyberspace. It will then attempt a first assessment of the advantages of such an approach to the problems of cyberspace over other approaches.

The following chapters will go on to explore in more detail the diplomatic approach to the problems outlined above, beginning with internet governance. This analysis draws parallels with the global issues, or new international security, agenda in physical space. It will distinguish between the governance of the internet's structure and the ongoing disagreements over the role of the Internet Corporation for Assigned Names and Numbers (ICANN) and the regulation of internet content and the behaviour of internet service providers. A key issue here is the conflict between those countries that want national regulation of the internet (internet sovereignty) and those who want to maintain a freer, global internet. The conclusions of the exploration of what a diplomatic approach looks like are applied to the challenges of internet governance. We examine what advantages a diplomatic approach may enjoy over other approaches – in particular, what alternative models of bottom-up regulation mediated through multilevel and heterogeneous networks of state and non-state actors would look like, and what the implications for the culture and practice of diplomacy would be. Finally, how can digital tools, especially blockchain technologies, support such regulatory innovation?

If the application of diplomacy to internet governance would seem obvious, if not inevitable, its value in reducing cyberconflict may be less. Can diplomacy reduce the threat of cyberwar, cyberespionage or cyberterrorism? We need to look at the relationship between cybersecurity and geopolitical agendas in physical space and the danger that they reinforce each other in promoting great-power conflict. The traditional security dilemma may pose even greater dangers in cyberspace and in physical space. The core argument is the importance of the diplomatic approach to reduce tensions and negotiate norms of behaviour which, without amounting to hard and fast guarantees of good conduct, provide constraints on states which, wanting to appear virtuous citizens of the international community in physical space, self-impose limitations on their behaviour in cyberspace.

Cybercrime imposes increasing costs on businesses and individuals. The existing strategy of depending on technical solutions against cyberattacks is the modern equivalent of the Maginot Line. Cyberattack eventually always prevails over cyberdefence, and private-sector companies are notoriously slow in identifying penetrations of their systems. We explore what a cyber business diplomacy approach (business diplomacy in cyberspace) might offer – in particular, by focusing on using diplomatic techniques to analyse a company's vulnerability to hackers and strategies to discourage or divert them, improving collaboration with other companies and government, and instituting both public diplomacy strategies to convince clients and suppliers that cyber breaches are the fault of the hacker, not the company, and strategies for improving the security culture within the company.

On a slightly different tack, we then need to look at the issue of algorithms and link them to both the crisis in public diplomacy and the reinforcement of echo chambers. We need to consider the manipulation of social media algorithms in information warfare and how a diplomatic approach might be used to secure a more cooperative approach from social media companies. There are also wider dangers of algorithms for diplomacy, both in terms of 'black boxes' in Big Data approaches to analysing international events, where analysts and policy-makers are unaware of the epistemological biases of the designer of the algorithm, and in terms of limiting the effectiveness of social-media-dependent public diplomacy. Does the diplomatic approach to cyberspace imply training diplomats how to game the algorithms of social media and search engines, or is there an alternative approach that could avoid such a confrontation?

This book concludes by considering what all this means for twenty-first-century diplomacy and diplomats. What are the challenges of operating simultaneously in physical and cyberspace? This forms part of a concept of 'hybrid diplomacy', where the diplomat must deal with multiple state and non-state actors, manage global issues and geopolitical agendas, and deal with international issues while remaining conscious of domestic political pressures. What are the changes needed in both the culture and the structure of foreign ministries, as well as the recruitment and training of diplomats? What also are the future challenges that cyberspace and other technologies are likely to throw up, and how can diplomacy and diplomats deal with them? In particular, what do technologies such as nanotechnology, quantum computing, artificial intelligence (AI) and machine learning mean for how diplomats function and the problems they must tackle? In the end, the book seeks to outline what an effective diplomacy for dealing with cyberspace might look like.

2

The Diplomat in Cyberspace

The argument of this book is that there is a diplomatic approach to the problems arising in cyberspace, and that this diplomatic approach can complement more technical or security-focused approaches. In other words, the application of diplomacy to the problems of cyberspace can bring benefits which extend beyond purely technical approaches. However, to sustain this we must have some idea about what this diplomatic procedure would look like. What is it about how a diplomat would approach cyberspace that distinguishes her from others working in the field, and what allows her to bring something new and useful to the party? It could be argued that cyberdiplomacy consists simply in negotiating about cyberspace problems rather than just developing new firewalls. But this is rather dull and adds little. I want to argue that there is a specifically diplomatic approach to international problems which could bring some real benefits in cyberspace. The ambition of this book is greater than simply to rehash, for cyberspace, Churchill's old saw that 'to jaw-jaw is always better than to war-war'.

Diplomats and Soldiers

It is not good enough simply to distinguish between a diplomatic and a military approach or a negotiating and confrontational or security-focused approach. It often seems that when the media talk about a diplomatic approach to an international problem – for example, North Korea's nuclear weapons programme – they mean no more than non-military means. But this is fundamentally to misunderstand the history and nature of diplomacy. Diplomacy and warfare are not opposite but complementary tools within the statesman's toolbox. A diplomatic approach to a problem does not necessarily pursue peace and international understanding. It is often said (so cited it is difficult to identify the original guilty party) that the outbreak of war always represents a failure of diplomacy, but this is true only when the objective of diplomacy is to avoid the outbreak of war. Sadly, history demonstrates not only that this is not always the case, but that there are many occasions when the objective of diplomacy was either to provoke a war or to create conditions more favourable for the conduct of a war. For example, Bismarck's foreign policy in the 1860s was aimed at provoking war with both Austria and France in the most favourable circumstances for securing Prussia's broader political objectives (the exclusion of Austria from German affairs and the forging of a unified German state dominated by Prussia).[1] While we excoriate the failure of Chamberlain's appeasement policy at Munich, at the time Hitler was furious at the failure of German diplomacy to deliver the war against Czechoslovakia that he wanted. Likewise, British diplomacy in 2003 was aimed not at avoiding war against Iraq but, rather, at securing a Security Council resolution which would give that war greater international legitimacy, and thus greater domestic support. Nor does diplomacy stop when war breaks out. During war diplomats continue their labours, seeking not only a negotiated outcome to a conflict (often not seeking that at all) but also to persuade neutrals to join their side or to strip allies from the enemy's side. In none of these cases are diplomacy and warfare opposed to each other or mutually exclusive. Rather, both form complementary parts of statecraft, aimed at securing the policy objectives set down by the government of the day. Nor is diplomacy always the junior partner in support of warfare. Conflict, or the threat of conflict, can be deployed in support of diplomacy, reinforcing the 'strength' of the diplomats' arguments. If this is true of diplomacy in physical space, it is likely to be equally true of diplomacy in cyberspace. Cyberdiplomacy and cyberwarfare are likely to be complementary sets of tools or processes for securing state and non-state actors' objectives in the virtual world.

Who are Diplomats?

If diplomacy cannot be defined either by simple opposition to warfare or as an activity inevitably devoted to the increase of international understanding, we need to find some other way of distinguishing it from other activities on the international stage. There is, of course, a large literature struggling with the definition of diplomacy. The issue has gained increased urgency with the plethora of new 'diplomacies' being propounded by practitioners and, especially, scholars. Books, academic papers and even university courses are being devoted to subjects such as sport diplomacy, gastro-diplomacy, science diplomacy and business diplomacy, to name but a few of the most egregious examples. Cyberdiplomacy can itself be seen as yet another example of this development. The increasing number of different new kinds of diplomacy poses two major problems. Firstly, in many of the studies of new diplomacy, there is confusion between agency, process and subject matter. It is not clear whether the new kind of diplomacy refers to new kinds of actors doing diplomacy, new tools available for a diplomat pursuing broader foreign policy strategies, or new areas where diplomacy can be deployed. For example, does sports diplomacy refer to a sportsman acting as a diplomat (e.g., a footballer being named a UNICEF goodwill ambassador), diplomats making use of sporting events to pursue broader foreign policy objectives (e.g., both Pyongyang and Seoul taking advantage of the Winter Olympics to reduce tensions on the Korean peninsula), or diplomacy being applied to problems arising in sport itself (e.g., negotiations to deal with Russia's exclusion from the Olympics because of drug abuse, or even the campaigns to host the Olympics themselves). In the case of cyberdiplomacy, it is clear that we are dealing with the third kind of activity, the application of diplomacy to a new area of subject matter – in this case, the problems arising in cyberspace (as opposed to digital diplomacy, which would be the second kind of activity, in which digital tools are used to promote diplomatic agendas).

A second, and in some ways more serious, problem is that excessive use of the word 'diplomacy' risks emptying the concept of any meaning. If everything is diplomacy, then nothing is. When discussion on diplomacy centres on how it is seen in common usage within families, diplomats themselves rightly question what value diplomatic studies may have for their profession. An austere approach to the definition of diplomacy is to insist that it is what is done by diplomats, and only by diplomats. If an activity is carried out by anyone who is not a diplomat, then by definition it cannot be diplomacy. Diplomats are then defined as those to whom the Vienna Convention on Diplomatic Relations applies. If you are not a diplomat accredited to a foreign state or an international organisation, as specified by the Vienna Convention, then you are not a diplomat, and what you do cannot be proper diplomacy. This approach has the benefit of simplicity and clarity and would disqualify the majority of new diplomacies. It would still allow us to talk about cyberdiplomacy, but only as the engagement with the problems of cyberspace by duly accredited diplomats. However, the definition is very narrow. It would exclude, for example, foreign ministry officials not serving in embassies abroad who are not accredited, and therefore are not covered by the Vienna Convention. It also does not reflect the developments in which the practice of international relations and foreign affairs in the twenty-first century has expanded to include a broad range of state and non-state actors, not all of whom are covered by the Vienna Convention (in this sense, it could even be argued that all the Vienna Conventions have been overtaken by developments and need review). It seems unnecessarily restrictive to rule out all of the state and non-state actors just because they are not duly accredited to foreign governments or international organisations.

At the same time, we would not want to include all participants, state or non-state actors, in international relations within the definition of diplomat. If we want to accept that some non-accredited actors do in fact behave like diplomats, but without emptying the concept of all meaning, we still need to find some way of distinguishing diplomatic behaviour from non-diplomatic behaviour. One approach which has been suggested has been to identify the activities undertaken by diplomats[2] and then argue that anybody undertaking these activities, at least in the context of international political and economic activities, is acting as a diplomat. It has been suggested that such diplomatic activities encompass national representation, information gathering and analysis, communication, networking, coalition building and negotiating. The trouble is that most of these activities are carried out, including in an international context, by actors whom we would not want to describe as diplomats, and who would not forgive us for so describing them. Many state and non-state actors indulge in international information gathering and analysis, among them journalists, intelligence agencies, academics and private-sector risk-management companies. All manner of state and

non-state actors negotiate in an international context, most
notably companies and transnational corporations. Even
if we limit the field to political negotiation (which would
exclude some activities of diplomats) we still find companies
and even NGOs engaged in negotiations with governments
or local militia groups. State and non-state actors also build
contact networks of influence and information (it would be
hard to imagine journalists functioning without them) and
construct coalitions among like-minded partners to secure
their objectives. Some coalitions constructed by non-state
actors will include governments (e.g., the coalition constructed by the Canadian mining sector to secure access to
the Bulgarian market, which involved other companies, the
Canadian government, the European Commission and even
environmental NGOs).[3] Indeed, virtually the only activity
unique to diplomats from this list would be the formal
representation of their country abroad (it could be argued
that we all represent our countries abroad informally, often
with devastating effects on national reputation). But if the
only unique attribute which distinguishes a diplomat from
other state and non-state actors in international relations is
the formal representation of his country abroad, we again
find ourselves limiting diplomats, and thus diplomacy, to
those formally accredited to foreign countries within the
terms of the Vienna Convention. Nor does it avail us to
argue that it is not the individual activities that mark out
the diplomat; rather, it is the combination of all these roles
in one person that distinguishes the diplomat from the
non-diplomat. Few diplomats perform all these roles at
the same time – indeed, some diplomats will not perform
all these roles in an entire diplomatic career.

The International Community of Diplomats

A more promising approach has been suggested by Paul
Sharp in his book *Diplomatic Theory of International*

Relations.[4] Building on the English School, and particularly Hedley Bull's concept of an international community of state,[5] Sharp suggests that there is also an international community of diplomats built around shared attitudes and ways of looking at the world. It suggests a certain commonality shared among diplomats but not by non-diplomat actors. The definition of a diplomat depends not on what she does, but the way in which she does it and the world view that her actions reflect. In the *Philosophical Investigations*[6] Wittgenstein discusses the different life forms (*Lebensformen*) that lie behind, and are reflected in, different language games. These life forms combine the shared attitudes, values and ways of engaging with the world that allow the rules of the language game to operate. In this sense, diplomacy can be seen as a kind of language game built on the shared life form, or way of being in the world, of diplomats. Becoming a diplomat means sharing in this diplomatic life form, based upon common attitudes and ways of seeing and interacting with international issues. In this interpretation of diplomacy, a non-state actor could be described as a diplomat provided that she shared in these common ways of acting with or thinking about the world. In terms of the subject matter of this book, this would suggest that cyberdiplomacy would describe how this diplomatic life form, or those who share it, would think about and engage with cyberspace. Any description of this diplomatic life form, and its implications for dealing with international problems, whether in physical or cyberspace, must inevitably be to some extent subjective and anecdotal. But it may nevertheless offer some interesting insights and, in particular, suggest some new ways of engaging with cyberspace.

The idea of a peculiarly diplomatic life form can be caught by the diplomatic dinner party. In theory, dinner parties consisting of diplomats from different countries, all stationed in a particular place, should be fascinating and entertaining experiences. After all, they bring together the different cultures and history not only of their own countries but also of the various countries in which they have been stationed during their careers. One would imagine interesting and exciting conversation from all sides. However, in fact, such dinners are frequently boring and unexciting. Conversations focus on such tedious issues as the living allowances paid by their home government, the ineptitude of local employees, and the injustices of the local government. Other exciting topics may include the difficulties of educating the children and the perils created by local driving habits. The reason such mundane topics dominate the conversation is that these are the issues that the diplomats and their spouses have in common (one of the rules of the diplomatic language game is to avoid even implicit competition over who has served in the most interesting posts). These shared experiences and preoccupations both illustrate an important aspect of diplomatic life and play an important role in allowing diplomats to perform their duties. Essentially diplomacy functions because diplomats have more in common with one another than they have with the country where they are stationed, or even with their own fellow nationals. A diplomat, separated from and protected from local society by privileges and immunity, never really belongs where she is posted. However, even after returning to their own countries, many diplomats never feel fully at home. They have learnt a way of looking at societies from the outside which they tend to apply even to their own country. Nevertheless it is this shared experience, and 'alienation' from their fellow men, that enables diplomats to operate. It permits them to keep talking to each other even when their fellow nationals, including their political leaders, are unable to do so. If there is a sense in which diplomats and diplomacy are related to international peace and understanding, it is that diplomats are able to keep talking to each other even when their countries are in conflict. The international community of diplomats is in some senses insulated against events and conflicts in the 'real world', for good or for ill. It is no accident that the UN headquarters in New York has so many obscure cafés and bars, where such conversations between diplomats can take place beyond the prying eyes of other diplomats and journalists.

Diplomatic Attributes

Accepting that this is necessarily subjective and anecdotal, we might consider some of the attributes shared by diplomats in general, and which may form part of the diplomatic life form. Diplomats in general see the world not in terms of moral black and white but, rather, in shades of grey. This does not mean that they are amoral, but they see the world as inherently complex and not amenable to simplification. However distasteful they may find it personally, they tend to maintain conversations with representatives of other countries, even in moments of tension or conflict, in ways that political leaders find more difficult. In part this reflects the greater obscurity of the diplomat, who, unlike the politician, rarely has to justify himself before his domestic public opinion. But it also reflects the existence of the international community of diplomats: as in a London club, you continue to talk to and socialise with other members of the club unless they are formally expelled. This may be why Western diplomats traditionally are cautious of pronouncements on the ethical element in foreign policy. Because of their recognition of the inherent complexity of the international environment, diplomats tend to think in terms of managing international crises and problems rather than resolving them. Instead of seeking optimal solutions, they are generally satisfied with outcomes that are 'good enough'. Unlike many politicians, especially those driven by morally self-righteous agendas, diplomats see the virtue of moderation and compromise. Central to good diplomacy is the virtue of empathy, the ability, and the desire, to see a problem through the eyes of a rival or even an enemy. This is essential to good foreign policy-making but is often, mistakenly, derided as sympathising with the foreigner. The need to see a problem from your opponent's point of view, and to understand both how he interprets your decisions and the decision that he is likely to take himself, would be recognised as essential by any chess player. But the attempt to explain how the rival or enemy interprets our policy decisions too often results in the diplomat being condemned as the foreigner's friend or as representing the interests of other countries rather than her own.

International Law

Even though this list of attributes is short, and surely open to question, it does allow us to consider further what a diplomatic approach to international affairs would be, rather than just talking instead of fighting. We can look at some of its implications for the practical business of diplomacy and then begin to consider how these might be applied to the problems arising in cyberspace. First of all, it implies an approach to international law that is neither as cynical as that of the realist nor as idealistic as that of the various kinds of liberals. Given its origin in the English School, this should not be surprising.[7] The diplomatic approach to international affairs does not consider international law as a series of norms that must be obeyed on all occasions, but nor does it envisage a Hobbesian anarchy of all against all. Rather, it sees international law as a social construct which provides limitations on the behaviour of the state through the desire of that state to remain a member of the international community. In as far as being a member of that international community requires states to pay at least lip service to the community's rules, then policy decisions will be conditioned by the need at least to appear legitimate. In this interpretation of international law, no government decides its foreign policy on the basis of what international law permits or demands. Rather, foreign policy is decided on the basis of national interest, and it must then be repackaged to appear to fall within the norms of international law. As I was told when a very junior diplomat by a foreign office legal advisor, do not ask what you are able to do according to international law, because the answer is nothing; rather, you should explain what you want to do, and the lawyer will then construct you a legal justification. While this may appear very cynical, it does amount to an effective, if limited, constraint on what states can do. The desire to remain, or become, a member of the international community means that states have to justify their actions within the accepted rules and norms. This does not mean that they will not do bad things, but that they will do them in such a way that they can claim some degree of legitimacy, even if credible only to themselves. For example, when Russia seized control of Crimea in 2014, Putin sought to legitimate this seizure of territory through a referendum on self-determination in which the people of Crimea demanded unification with Russia. It may not have convinced political or public opinion in the West, but, in the Kremlin's eyes at least, it mirrored the independence referendum in Kosovo and maintained Russia's claim to legitimacy and membership of the international community. Even more important, the same desire to remain within the norms of the international community may have constrained Putin from the temptation to seize the rest of Ukraine. Militarily this may have been possible. But it would have been impossible to justify in any interpretation of international law and would have left Russia beyond the pale of the international community. There is an important corollary here. If the desire to remain within the international community of states acts as an effective, if limited, constraint on state behaviour, being cast out of that community removes the constraint. Any state expelled from the international community, with no realistic hope of returning (or where the price of return is set too high), will not feel constrained by the need to appear to conform with international law, and will accordingly become a more dangerous, and more unpredictable, threat to international order.

Diplomatic Socialisation

A second important implication, which flows from this account of international law, is the importance of socialisation, both of states and of their diplomats. Diplomacy functions by socialising states and individuals into the international communities. If states (and their leaders) want to be seen to be respecting international law so as to remain members of the international community, then the process of bringing states into that community, and giving them an incentive for respecting its norms, becomes central to the diplomatic approach to international relations. This process of socialisation can be illustrated by the various revolutionary states in the twentieth century. When the nascent Soviet Union first sent its ambassadors abroad at the end of the First World War, their task was to foment revolution in the countries where they were deployed. They were emphatically not members of the international community of diplomats.[8] Rather than negotiating with their host governments or developing networks of influence and information to shape attitudes towards the Soviet Union, they networked with trade unions and left-wing parties to overthrow them. But gradually the need to deal with foreign governments over trade and wider economic relations normalised Soviet diplomacy, and Soviet diplomats were gradually socialised into the international diplomatic community. By the 1930s, Ivan Maisky was serving in London as a highly effective diplomat in pursuit of Soviet interests and as an early master of public diplomacy.[9] Similarly, during the Cultural Revolution, Chinese diplomats abroad acted as agents of Maoist ideology, stirring up dissent in local Chinese diasporas (even as their counterparts in the Foreign Ministry planned the burning of the British embassy in Beijing). Yet, when I arrived in China twenty years later as a junior diplomat, we were already dealing with fully socialised diplomats who, in appearance, at least, shared much of the view of, and manner of interacting with, the world of their Western counterparts (although they were rather better negotiators). Similar stories of socialisation or normalisation could be told of the representatives of revolutionary Islamic republics such as Iran or Libya. As time passed, the diplomats of these countries lost interest in spreading their Islamic revolutions and devoted more time to traditional diplomatic activities, ending up scarcely distinguishable from other professional diplomats.

New Actors

The socialisation aspect of diplomacy and the inclusion of a broader range of actors within the international diplomatic community is likely to be equally important in the twenty-first century. As we have already seen, new agendas and new digital technologies have multiplied the number of state and non-state actors participating in international affairs. The question of whether or not these actors, especially non-state actors, are doing diplomacy is not only of theoretical interest. If, as suggested above, the existence of an international community of diplomats has been a key part of how diplomacy functions, allowing conversations to be maintained when otherwise there would be no means of moderating conflict, what are the implications of the entry of non-diplomats for the management of international relations? If the tendency of diplomats to see the world in shades of grey and to seek 'sufficient' outcomes has helped maintain global stability, will the entrance of non-state actors who see the world more in black and white and who insist on optimal solutions generate instability? The question of whether there is something called NGO diplomacy or business diplomacy is converted into whether business executives or NGO activists will become socialised as diplomats (as the representatives of revolutionary regimes were in the past). If so, then the task of multi-stakeholder diplomacy, in which diplomats must deal with a broad range of state and non-state actors, is simplified by gradually converting them into diplomats. If not, not only are there implications for the management of international issues and global stability, but diplomats must increasingly learn how to engage with actors who do not share their view of, or way of engaging with, the world. To some extent they have always done this, with mixed success, when working with or analysing the intentions of politicians or policy formers. But it is likely to become a more central part of their function.

Diplomacy in Cyberspace

The discussion is this chapter serves to define better the key argument of the book. It is not simply asserting that governments, and non-state actors, should negotiate over the problems of cyberspace as well as implementing technical security measures. It does do that: technical security measures are necessary, but not sufficient. Governments to some extent are negotiating over some aspects of cyberspace, although they could certainly do more. But this book goes further. It argues that we need to build an international community of diplomats in cyberspace who can work to socialise other state and non-state actors to join that community. This international community of diplomats will also have to learn how to deal with state and non-state actors who do not share their diplomatic world view. Developing a multi-stakeholder diplomatic capability will be as important in cyberspace as in physical space. At the moment there is no such capability. Diplomats and diplomacy as characterised above are absent, as is international law or widely accepted norms of behaviour. Although attempts have been made to assert that existing international law also applies in cyberspace, key countries such as China and Russia have backed away from commitment.[10] In effect, cyberspace is like some Hobbesian world of anarchy in which all struggle against all. If international law operates in physical space through the desire of states to belong to the international community (supported by the socialisation of their diplomats into the international diplomatic community), and to be seen as such, at least in their own eyes, it is likely to operate in cyberspace in the same way. The task of cyberdiplomacy becomes the construction of an international community in cyberspace paralleling that in physical space, to which states (and non-state actors) will want to belong, and consequently whose norms they will want to be seen to follow. In doing so, the attributes of the diplomatic life form described above will be key: a view of the world in shades of grey that involves a readiness to engage with all manner of actors; a capacity for empathy that enables diplomats to see the actions of their own governments through the eyes of others; a willingness to accept good enough outcomes rather than insist on optimal solutions; an acceptance that problems at a global level can often only be managed, not solved; and the ability to construct multilevel and heterogeneous networks of state and non-state actors.

3

Regulating Cyberspace

The Structure of Cyberspace

Although in some senses cyberspace remains anarchic, and there is open debate as to whether existing international law applies there, in other senses there is already considerable regulation, as well as international debate about developing more. This is inevitable. Without some rules and regulations, at least at the technical level, the internet itself would not function. While these technical rules in themselves are not especially controversial, who polices them, and how, generates considerable debate. Internet governance refers to the management of the world's internet resources. That management can be purely technical, but it can also relate to issues surrounding data protection, encryption and even content. Who manages the world's internet resources, and according to what principles, will shape not only the internet (and cyberspace) but also wider international and domestic society. It is hardly surprising that it is a highly controversial topic or that, as a controversial international issue, it should offer scope for applying the diplomatic approach outlined in the previous chapter.

Cyberspace is often said to operate as an inverted four-layer pyramid.[1] The first, bottom, layer is the hardware layer. This is the physical network of fibre optic cables linking the different internet service providers (ISPs) and their internet exchange points. The second layer is the logic layer – the level at which computer code decides how the internet functions and how information is distributed through it. In this layer, for example, transmission control protocols (TCPs) ensure information gets sent in the right direction, internet protocol numbers (IPs) identify computers linked to the internet, and the domain name system (DNS) provides the website addresses as well as the top-level domains (TLDs – .com, .net, .de, etc.). The data layer describes the information flowing around the internet. This includes emails, webpage content and blogs, as well as videos, which account for between 65 and 85 per cent of internet traffic. It is where we share, often unwittingly, our own data about ourselves and others. The final, uppermost, layer is the social layer, which is where humans interact on the internet. As the US Cyber Command (USCYBERCOM) puts it, cyberspace consists of 'the physical network level, the logical network level, the cyber persona level and ... people'.[2]

Internet governance issues arise at all layers of the internet, although the most pressing and controversial among them tend to arise at the upper three layers. Some authors have sought to divide these into technical governance and policy governance. The idea is that the issues at the physical and logical layers are essentially technical, ensuring that the hardware and navigating systems of the internet are working correctly. These are matters that can be left to the engineers and software engineers. Governance questions at the data and social layers, however, are more complicated and do not have straightforward solutions. For example, data protection and webpage content lie well beyond the purview of engineers and need more political debate and decision. According to this schema, cyberdiplomacy would have scope to operate only at the data or social layers and would not be needed at the physical or logic layers. However, this clear distinction between technical and policy matters is profoundly misguided. All internet governance issues are political and reflect deep divisions of opinion about what the internet should be and how it should operate. There is a parallel with nuclear weapons. Controversies concerning nuclear weapons issues cannot be divided into technical and policy questions, as the technical and engineering design of nuclear weapons has a profound impact on nuclear strategy and policy debates. As a consequence, strategy and politics reach deep down into the technical discussions. Likewise, decisions taken at the physical or logic layers of the internet (e.g., net neutrality, the management of the domain name system (DNS) or the physical protection of internet cables) have profound implications for the shape and functioning of the data and social layers. It is hardly surprising, then, that debates about all layers of internet governance are highly politicised and, in as far as they are international, their management requires diplomatic skills and techniques.

All international institutions reflect the geopolitical balance of power at the moment of their creation. In a sense, the structures and culture of international institutions freeze that balance of power at the moment of creation, and institutional inertia makes such structures and cultures difficult to change. As relative geopolitical power shifts over time, the international institutions can become ever more remote from everyday realities, with negative impact on their ability to engage effectively with current events. The prime example is the United Nations. No one today would propose either Britain or France as permanent members of the Security Council – their presence reflects their 'great power' status in 1945. But the rules are so written that they can veto their own removal, thus effectively preventing any radical Security Council reform. Likewise, the UN Charter is written for a world where the major international security concern was interstate warfare. It is not fit for

purpose for a world where the major concerns are civil
wars and humanitarian crises, on neither of which does it
provide for intervention. The General Assembly has adopted
a resolution on the responsibility to protect (R2P). But
General Assembly resolutions are not binding and cannot in
themselves authorise military interventions. Such interventions can still only be authorised under Chapter 7 by the
Security Council and must be couched in the language of
a threat to international peace and security. The revisionist
policies increasingly being adopted by China and Russia
make such Chapter 7 resolutions as unlikely as they were
in the Cold War.

In many ways the Internet is also an international institution that reflects the geopolitical balance of power of the
moment of its creation. Although the early stages of its
development occurred in the Cold War, the global internet as we know it today was a product of the 1990s. Its
birth coincided with an unprecedented period of US global
domination following the collapse of the Soviet Union and
before the rise of China. The culture and structure of the
internet reflected this period of US hegemony (or the 'uni-
polar' moment). American values of free trade and freedom
of expression were difficult to resist at a time when Francis
Fukuyama had proclaimed the end of history and the inevi-
tability of a globalised liberal market economy. It is not
surprising that the other international institution founded
in that decade was the World Trade Organization (WTO),
created to enshrine a US-dominated international free trade
in an ever more globalised economy. It is hard to imagine
either the WTO or a global internet being established either
a decade earlier or a decade later. If the technology for the
internet had been sufficiently developed in the 1980s, there
would surely have been a NATO internet, a Soviet internet,
and possibly Chinese and non-aligned internets as well, all
incompatible with each other. Likewise, had the technology
been developed now, there would likely be a US internet,
an EU internet, a Chinese internet, a Russian internet and

perhaps an Indian internet. Communication and the flow of information between the internets would be limited, and other countries would decide to which internet they wanted to accede (or create their own). Control of the different internets would be essentially national (except the regional control of the EU) and would reflect perceptions of national interest. In case this seems far-fetched, the last decade has seen a tendency towards regional free trade groups, where geopolitical considerations weigh as heavily as commercial ones, whether President Obama building on the North American Free Trade Agreement (NAFTA) with the Trans-Pacific Partnership (TPP) or the Transatlantic Trade and Investment Partnership (TTIP), President Putin trying to impose the Eurasian Economic Community (EEC) as a counterweight to the European Union (EU), or China pushing the 'Belt and Road Initiative' (BRI).

Internet Governance

The extent to which the internet reflects the already non-existent geopolitical balance of the 1990s is reflected in the divisions over internet governance between the 'free internet nations' and the 'cyber sovereignty advocates'.[3] The free internet nations, essentially the US and its allies, seek to maintain the internet as it is, global and largely free from government interference. In as far as the internet must be regulated, especially at the physical and logical level, they advocate a multi-stakeholder model, which includes states, the private sector, civil society, international governmental organisations, the technical community and academics. The cyber sovereignty advocates, led by Russia and China, seek to recover the territory conceded in the 1990s by establishing state sovereignty over cyberspace within their borders. Although they pay lip service to the multi-stakeholder model, they believe that internet governance and regulation should essentially be brought within existing governmental international organisations (e.g., the UN or the International Telecommunications Union – ITU). At least one author has suggested that the confrontation between the free internet nations and the cyber sovereignty advocates reflects the confrontation between the US and the Soviet Union, and their respective allies, during the Cold War.[4] The increasingly authoritarian nature of the regimes among the cyber sovereignty advocates, especially in Russia and China, implies that the desire for cyber sovereignty reflects an aspiration for government control over the internet and increased censorship of content. At the same time, the support of the free internet nations for an internet unfettered by government intervention is not unqualified. The revelations by Edward Snowden of the extent of internet surveillance by the US National Security Agency (NSA) and other Western government agencies have severely undermined their credibility. Some of their policy positions on internet governance issues (e.g., net neutrality, encryption or webpage content) also questions their commitment to a 'free internet' and may offer hostages to the cyber sovereignty advocates.

The difficulties and controversies of internet governance can be seen at the logic layer, where the 'hot' governance topics include the Internet Corporation for Assigned Names and Numbers (ICANN) and net neutrality.[5] ICANN is a unique organisation in global governance and a typical product of the period of US-dominated unipolarity. A non-governmental not-for-profit corporation incorporated in California, it was created in 1998 and contracted by the US Department of Commerce to manage internet names and addresses (the so called IANA – Internet Assigned Numbers Authority). In 2014 the Department of Commerce announced it would give up the IANA role and no longer contract it to ICANN, and in 2016 this aspect was transferred to ICANN in its own right. ICANN is run by a board of fifteen directors, nominated in a bottom-up process by a range of specialist bodies. There is no formal governmental representation on the board, although there is a governmental advisory committee without voting rights. The non-governmental, semi-commercial and expert driven nature of ICANN reflects the culture of information technology at the time of the internet's birth. It has a distinct flavour of Silicon Valley. But it is anathema to many governments, who believe that a global information technology network as important as the internet should enjoy some form of governmental regulation. They have argued that ICANN's non-governmental nature is accidental and that its functions should be brought within an intergovernmental international organisation such as the ITU – unsurprisingly, the ITU agrees. Opponents of this view argue that the non-governmental nature of ICANN is central to the development of a global internet and that all regulation or governance of the internet must take account of all its stakeholders, including the private sector, civil society and technical experts.

For now, those arguing that ICANN should remain unchanged have held the line, but other governance issues surrounding ICANN and its IANA function remain in debate. One is centred on online identities and whether some domain names should be reserved for geographical regions or political entities. It has arisen over .amazon, which the online retailer Amazon wishes to claim but which Brazil is arguing must belong to the Amazon region as a regional equivalent of a country-code top level domain (ccTLD). Such arguments embroil ICANN once more in the arguments between those who see the internet as essentially non-governmental and non-geographical and those who wish to reassert national sovereignty in cyberspace. A second issue focuses on ICANN's status and location. Even if they accept ICANN's existence, many governments argue it should no longer be physically located in the United States (especially as it is no longer contracted by the US Department of Commerce) or incorporated under California state law (as it is a global entity). If ICANN is to remain in the US, they maintain, it should be accorded the same immunities and privileges as other international organisations. In many ways this is an attempt to bring ICANN into intergovernmental structures by the back door. If ICANN is to be granted diplomatic immunities and privileges in accordance with the Vienna Convention, then it effectively becomes an international organisation, and at least some of its employees acquire diplomatic status. In the longer term this may attract broader support, and be harder to argue against, than direct incorporation into the ITU.[6]

In another area of the logic layer, the US may have taken a decision which further undermines the standing of the free internet nations. The end-to-end (e2e) principle, that all innovation on the network should take place at the ends rather than in the centre, was established early in the development of the internet. This is sometimes rephrased as the principle of net neutrality: that all traffic on the internet should be treated the same, and that telecommunications companies that provide the hardware over which the data flows should not be allowed to differentiate between different kinds of traffic (for example, treat some as a lower priority or charge extra for VIP service). The argument behind the principle of net neutrality is that the internet is a public utility, and internet providers should not be able to interfere with how it operates. The US Federal Communications Commission (FCC) in February 2015 confirmed that it would enforce net neutrality and that it would regulate internet providers as public utility companies. The telecommunications companies that provide the internet complained that this was unfair. The internet media companies that sell content on the internet, such as Netflix or YouTube, use increasing bandwith and make the lion's share of the profits but contribute little to the development of the internet's infrastructure. Abandoning net neutrality would enable the internet providers to charge service providers like YouTube and Netflix more for transporting their data, effectively taxing them for their greater bandwidth usage. After an extensive lobbying campaign, the FCC reversed its decision in December 2017 and announced it would no longer protect net neutrality. This decision is now being challenged in the courts by a series of user groups.[7] However, whatever the outcome, the FCC decision strengthens the arguments of those who claim that the US is interested only in the interests of its telecommunications companies and effectively wants to privatise the internet. It will also strengthen the arguments of those who claim that the internet, as a global public good, cannot be left to the vagaries of US commercial policy and that its regulation should be by an international intergovernmental body. The Trump administration may discover, in yet another area of policy, that, by undermining international institutions through which the United States has led the world, it has undermined the country's ability to influence key global decision-making.

Data Protection

The major governance issues at the data level centre on the use and protection of data. Two issues in particular will continue to be the focus of debate: data protection/ privacy and encryption are, of course, related. The internet has generated enormous quantities of data, much of it personal. Individuals, whether through the use of social media or credit or shop loyalty cards, are constantly uploading personal information into cyberspace, much of it unwittingly. As few read the terms and conditions of the online services they are using (typically dozens, or even hundreds, of pages of small print), few are aware of the uses to which their data can be put. Social media companies such as Facebook, Twitter, Google or YouTube depend on this data to secure marketing revenues. The algorithms which they use to analyse it to ensure advertising tailored to each user are central to their business models (as we will see in chapter

6, these algorithms pose their own problems for diplomacy). Edward Snowden revealed the extent to which US
and other intelligence agencies collect this data, in theory
as part of the war against international terrorism. More
recent revelations about the use of Facebook data by the
UK-based company Cambridge Analytica to help profile
voters, and so target them with tailored campaign material
in the 2016 US presidential elections, has provoked new
concerns about how individuals' online data is used.[8] There
is also the problem of the theft of such data for criminal
use (which we will look at in more detail in chapter 5).

The European Union has responded to these concerns
about the privacy of citizens' data with the General Data
Protection Regulation (GDPR), which came into force in
May 2018.[9] The GDPR requires internet companies to
secure the agreement of users whenever their data is used
beyond the legitimate business purposes of the contract.
In other words, companies can only collect data that is
strictly needed for the performance of their contract with
the client. If they want to use data for other purposes, such
as data mining or marketing, they will need the explicit
and separate consent of each individual or organisation.
The GDPR foresees penalties of fines of up to €20 million,
or 4 per cent of a company's global annual revenue. It
applies not only to the territory of the EU but also to the
management of the data of EU citizens wherever that data
is being processed. This means that companies processing
data even outside the EU must be aware of whether any of
the information was provided by EU citizens. The GDPR
calls into question the business model of a broad range
of internet or social media companies. But the renewed
furore provoked by the revelations of Facebook's witting or
unwitting collaboration with Cambridge Analytica means
that they will receive scant public sympathy or support.

The GDPR is another example of a trend in twenty-first-
century international regulation: the use of extra-territorial
legislation. Countries, or regional organisations such as

the EU, realise that securing consensus or agreement to new regulatory frameworks at a global level is increasingly difficult in a multipolar world (we will look at this again in the context of global governance). At the same time they have recognised that the attractiveness of their domestic markets provides indirect ways of constructing global rule sets that apply not only to their own companies but also to foreign companies that wish to operate in their markets. The main area in which this has functioned so far has been anti-corruption. The US Foreign Corrupt Practices Act (FCPA)[10] applies not only to the operations of US companies anywhere in the world but also to the operations anywhere in the world of foreign companies with a presence in the US. In other words, if a foreign company wants to operate in the United States, it opens up all its operations all around the world to the scrutiny of the US Justice Department. This is not theoretical. The US Justice Department has successfully prosecuted foreign companies for corrupt practices in third countries (the British Bribery Act has similar extra-territorial effect). By applying the GDPR to the management of the data of EU citizens wherever that data is processed in the world, the EU is following suit: any company processing such data anywhere in the world that wants to have any kind of presence in the EU will have to abide by the regulation. The European Commission calculates, almost certainly correctly, that its internal market is sufficiently attractive to internet data management and processing companies that it can pull this off. The EU will effectively set the data protection standards for the rest of the world, or at least those parts of it that want to do business with the EU and EU citizens.

The problem of encryption arises from the conflict between the need to keep data, including that of individual citizens, secure and the need to protect citizens against the broader threats of crime and terrorism. Everyday technologies such as mobile telephones increasingly encrypt their activities to increase the security and privacy of their users. This applies to software applications such as WhatsApp (which is one of the reasons for its popularity with diplomats in multinational negotiations, who can use it for secure communication with colleagues, protected from allies or even rivals). The levels of encryption are very high, if not necessarily unbreakable. This poses problems for law-enforcement and intelligence agencies, who want real-time access to the communications of criminals and terrorists (and foreign intelligence officers). Encryption of everyday devices denies them this easy access. As a consequence they have put pressure on tech companies and software designers either to grant them one-off access in specific cases by providing the key to the encryption or to install back doors in the encryption software that would allow them to gain access to someone's device or application when required (presumably governed by some sort of system of warrants). But this is controversial, even within government. Those responsible for cybersecurity warn that back doors allowing access for the good guys also allow access to the bad guys – cybercriminals and foreign governments – intent on stealing data. Those in foreign ministries responsible for promoting democracy and human rights abroad complain that undermining end-to-end encryption on mobile devices could put dissidents at risk from authoritarian regimes. Those responsible for exports in trade ministries point out that even the suspicion that companies are building back doors into devices limits the opportunities for exports, with foreign governments and publics concerned about the scope for espionage and data theft. The US House of Representatives, for example, is discussing banning US government agencies from using Huawei and ZTE phones and equipment because of concerns that the Chinese intelligence services have built in this kind of back door which would allow them to access US government data. Added to these specific concerns are the broader worries about privacy and the protection of personal data. Although various technical solutions have been mooted (as far back as the 1990s, the NSA proposed the Clipper chip as a way of guaranteeing access to online systems to fight crime and terrorism), ultimately this is about the balance between security of data and broader security, which will need to be debated by the various state and non-state stakeholders concerned.[11]

Cryptocurrencies such as Bitcoin and Ether, and the blockchain technologies that support them, have generated a whole literature of their own. We do not need to go into the technicalities of how they function (although we will return to blockchains later). Our focus is on the growing calls for greater regulation of cryptocurrencies,[12] which is adding yet another issue to the internet governance agenda. Initial concerns were focused on the use of cryptocurrencies in the 'dark web' (obscure areas of the web that have to be accessed through special servers and browsers) to buy drugs, weapons and other illegal products. This was essentially a law and order problem. The success of the FBI in taking down the Silk Road drugs emporium showed that operations on the dark web were not as securely anonymous as many thought.[13] However, a series of wider regulatory concerns are emerging about cryptocurrencies. The digital mining process by which transactions are validated and new crypto coins created is profligate in its use of energy. This has led crypto miners to move operations to countries with low electricity prices, which in turn has raised concerns about the increased demands on the local electricity supply, especially in countries dependent on coal for electricity production such as China, where cryptocurrency mining has environmental implications. In February 2018, such concerns led China to halt trading in virtual currencies, ban initial coin offerings and shut down mining. Cryptocurrency mining seems to have shifted to Canada and Iceland, where the electricity is not only cheap but from renewable sources. But concerns are growing too in Iceland, where the local energy company calculates that during 2018 the consumption of energy by cryptocurrency mining will outstrip domestic home consumption, pushing up prices for consumers. These energy demands of cryptocurrencies are driving calls for greater regulation from environmental and consumer groups. Central banks are also getting in on the act. Concerned both that the wild swings in the value of cryptocurrencies, driven by speculation, could impact negatively on the real economy and by the increased use of cryptocurrencies for financial crime such as fraud, money laundering and tax evasion, they are exploring new regulatory frameworks. But cryptocurrencies are not all negative. Like encrypted communication devices, they have helped support human rights and dissidents under authoritarian regimes. As shown by China's efforts to shut down Bitcoin, the regulation of cryptocurrencies cannot be achieved at a national level but will need some form of international collaboration.

Internet Content

Regulatory issues at the social or human layer currently focus on controlling undesirable content and regulating the activities of service providers. Concerns about social media content, whether support for Islamic extremism or promoting racial or gender hatred and violence, have grown on political agendas, particularly in the US and Europe. These link to worries about the use of social media by Islamic terrorist groups to recruit new members but also about the impact of such extremist content on the democratic process – for example, the 2016 US presidential election and the Brexit referendum (we'll look at the weaponisation of information by governments and their surrogates in the next chapter). 'Fake news' – the use of social media to spread deliberately misleading, untrue and malicious content – became one of the buzzwords of 2017. Social media companies were, to a large extent, caught out by these growing public and political concerns. The procedures they had put in place themselves to control extremist content were repeatedly shown to be lacking. Neither algorithms nor human controllers seemed adequate to identifying and taking down unacceptable material, while the definition of what is unacceptable is inevitably contested. The internet companies have promised to do better, and Facebook, Microsoft, Twitter and YouTube have formed a Global Internet Forum to Counter Terrorism. But there are calls for governments to be more active. Germany has already adopted legislation that would fine internet companies with more than 2 million German users which do not take down unacceptable content in less than 24 hours. France has announced legislation to tackle fake news. The UK has warned internet companies that they will be penalised if they do not find a solution for violent extremist content. But the regulation of unacceptable content poses three major problems for governments. National government action is of limited value without wider international collaboration. The definition of what is unacceptable content and what is an unacceptable restriction on freedom of speech is controversial and likely to vary from country to country. There was uproar recently when a Spanish student was charged for tweeting a joke about the death of Franco's prime minister Carrera Blanco. Finally, the desire to remove unacceptable content from social media risks aligning previously free internet nations with the cyber sovereignty advocates, who have their own reasons for wanting to control social media content.[14]

Services

The final governance issue we will look at is the regulation of providers of 'Over the Top' (OTT) services. National telecommunications companies provide the physical infrastructure and information networks on which the internet operates. 'Over the top' of this physical infrastructure has developed a thick web of interrelationships between users and service providers. In a sense, most people and companies are both users and service providers, using services provided by one group of providers to offer services to another group of users (e.g., using a web-hosting service to create a website which sells products or services to others or a social media platform to provide family photographs for grandparents). One group of service providers are of particular concern. They have near monopoly status, and they offer services also provided at a national level, for example by national telecommunications companies. But they escape national regulatory frameworks. Skype and WhatsApp, for instance, like national telecommunications companies, offer mobile telephony and messaging services. Unlike national telecommunications companies, however, they are not regulated at national level for issues such as taxation, quality of service, accessibility, portability or protection of data. The question of taxation in relation to online retailers is particularly thorny, as companies such as Amazon have taken advantage of tax laws designed for another world to reduce their tax burdens. As citizens become increasingly aware of how online service providers operate, the pressure for some form of effective regulation will grow.[15]

New Approaches to Regulation

The standard model for introducing new regulatory frameworks over the last fifty years has been either through intergovernmental negotiation in the context of an existing international organisation or through creating a new organisation. Thus the UN Law of the Sea was negotiated within the framework of the United Nations, while the World Trade Organization was created to regulate global trade. Regulation was therefore essentially an intergovernmental and top-down process. There are reasons for believing that this approach to global governance will not function as easily in the twenty-first century. There is strong resistance from the free internet countries to using existing international organisations such as the UN or the ITU for internet governance. Allowing either organisation to take the lead would be seen as essentially gifting the game to the cyber sovereignty advocates, who would use the inter-governmental culture and structures of these institutions to promote governmental control of cyberspace. Allowing existing international organisations to govern the internet would also arouse the ire and opposition of internet user groups, internet-related NGOs, and the various technician groups who maintain and operate the architecture of the internet. But, for reasons that extend beyond the internet and depend more on the nature of international systems, it is not likely that it will be possible to create new international organisations with global reach.

If international institutions reflect, or freeze, the geo-political power balance of the moment of their creation, they tend to be created only when there exists a global hegemon or following hegemonic war. Thus the ITU itself was created in 1865 at a time of British relative hegemony. The International Labour Organization was created, along with the League of Nations, following the blood-letting of the First World War, while the UN and its specialised agencies were established after the Second World War. The Bretton Woods institutions – the International Monetary Fund (IMF) and World Bank – and the General Agreement on Tariffs and Trade (GATT) were also set up after the Second World War but did not become truly global until the end of the Cold War, when US hegemony was clear and Washington was able to impose its economic view of the world through the conversion of the GATT into the World Trade Organization. The reason that international organisations tend to be created under these two condi-tions is that they require a sufficient consensus of values and ideas on how the world should be structured, either generated by the horror of hegemonic war or accepted from the hegemon, or both. These conditions do not hold in the increasingly multipolar world of the twenty-first century. New international organisations have been established by the BRICS (Brazil, Russia, India, China and South Africa), but they do not have global reach or regulatory functions. Indeed, much of the attraction of China's Asian Infrastructure Investment Bank (AIIB) is that it does not aspire to the regulatory or tutelage roles of the IMF and World Bank. Instead of a growing consensus on values or rules for governing international political and economic relations, the existing rule sets seem to be fragmenting. The lack of consensus on internet governance can be seen in the confrontation between the free internet countries and cyber sovereignty advocates and their radically different ideas of how the internet should be governed. Even in areas where they appear to agree, for example the regulation of internet content, their objectives are radically different: to preserve the internet as a safe space for free debate versus to limit and control the access to information of their citizens.[16] The importance of non-state actors in the design, management (ICANN), maintenance and operation of the internet, including technicians and user groups as well as companies and NGOs, further decreases the likelihood of top-down regulation or governance through a new international intergovernmental organisation. Attempts to force the internet within this type of governance model risks only further fragmenting debate, and even the internet itself, as the cyber sovereignty advocates increasingly carve their cyber territory away from the rest of the internet.

An alternative approach is an increased use of extra-territorial legislation, following the example of the EU's GDPR. Countries (or regional organisations such as the EU) with sufficiently attractive online markets can leverage that market attraction to establish national legislation that effectively has international impact. Social media companies must now effectively apply the GDPR to all their data if they want to operate in the EU (unless they are confident that they can clearly distinguish between EU citizen and non-EU citizen data). However, there is no guarantee that equally attractive online markets will adopt compatible legislation. In the case of anti-corruption, US and UK legislation is broadly consistent. It is not hard for companies to comply with both. But would that be true of data protection regulations? While the GDPR insists on protecting the data of EU citizens, China insists that the data of its citizens be shared with the government. China's Social Credit System,[17] due to be rolled out in 2020, will collect data on Chinese citizens, including those living abroad, to give them 'credit ratings' which will impact their access to employment or privileges. It is difficult to see how companies could simultaneously satisfy European and Chinese data requirements without the expensive process of distinguishing between their European and Chinese clients and treating their data differently. Even that may be insufficient for a Chinese citizen resident in the EU, whose data may be subject to both sets of regulations. The use of extra-territorial legislation risks regulatory chaos for companies and further fragmentation of the internet.

If internet governance cannot be top-down, a better approach may be bottom-up (indeed, this may be true of all new regulatory frameworks in the twenty-first century and prove a feature of multipolar global systems). Rather than governments meeting to negotiate regulatory frameworks and rule sets which are imposed through new international organisations, and which state and non-state actors must accept, the regulatory process starts in conversations between state and non-state actors at the local level. The debates on internet governance are mediated through global networks of state and non-state actors facilitated by the very cyberspace they are discussing, and taking advantage of encryption to guarantee the safety and frankness of their conversations. These networked and multilevel debates allow participants to generate coalitions based on shared preferred outcomes which cut across the distinctions between state and non-state actors. Local-level agreements can be progressively built up into broader regulatory frameworks, which acquire authority through the number and range of their adherents. By eschewing claims of exclusivity or universality from the beginning, such a gradual bottom-up approach minimises the risks of fragmentation or massive initial disagreements that simply block progress. There is a precedent for such an approach: the climate change talks that ultimately resulted in the Paris Agreement on climate change. While much of the early debate on climate change was between scientists, taking advantage of networks originally created to promote scientific exchanges across the barrier of the Iron Curtain, these evolved into multilevel and heterogeneous debates between state and non-state actors (including companies and NGOs as well as scientists) mediated through global contact networks. These gradually allowed the forming of equally heterogeneous coalitions of state and non-state actors centred on preferred outcomes rather than shared ideologies or world views. These coalitions were clearly visible during the Paris climate talks and played a key role in the final agreement.

The regulation of cyberspace through a bottom-up process mediated through global networks of state and non-state actors has implications for the role of diplomats. Rather than negotiating new regulatory frameworks with other diplomats, they will need to engage with the full range of state and non-state actors or stakeholders (this is often referred to as multi-stakeholder diplomacy). The non-state stakeholders will include a broad range of companies, not just internet or tech companies (as we will discuss in chapter 5, in the modern digital ecosystem, all companies are tech companies), academics, technicians, NGOs, hacker collectives and less formal user groups. Although diplomats will seek to secure the policy objectives of their governments, they will have to do so through cooperation and encouragement rather than fiat and coercion. They will need to deploy their networking and coalition-building skills as much as their negotiating skills. Working through surrogates will often be more effective than acting themselves as protagonists. As public diplomatists have long known, surrogates are more credible and effective advocates than diplomats themselves. In regulatory multi-stakeholder diplomacy, diplomats will need to deploy many of the techniques commonly thought of as belonging to public diplomacy, engaging as much with foreign publics as with foreign governments (the public in general is another stakeholder in internet governance, and a major one), using conferences, workshops and other types of events, on- or offline, to promote debates in which the ideas of their governments can hold sway. In this kind of multi-stakeholder diplomacy, the diplomat is more a facilitator than a protagonist, a diplomatic entrepreneur who identifies and promotes potential relationships and conversations between other state and non-state actors. The ultimate objective is to use the networks she develops to construct coalitions which share many if not all of the preferred outcomes of her government. These coalitions then become the agents advancing the internet governance agenda. If traditional bilateral diplomacy was like chess, in which each player sought to capture the centre of the board to be able to effect his strategies, multi-stakeholder diplomacy in internet governance is more like Chinese chess (Go), or *weiqi*, where the player operates indirectly and discreetly around the margins to secure her objectives – more Sun Tzu than Clausewitz.

Reverting to the previous chapter on the nature of the diplomat, one of the major features posited was the international community of diplomats and the importance of socialisation within it. One of the key issues of multi-stakeholder diplomacy, whether in relation to internet governance or more broadly, is whether diplomats will be able to socialise non-state actors within the international community of diplomats. Other characteristics we identified of diplomats was a certain amorality that sees the world in shades of grey, rather than black and white, and a tendency towards accepting outcomes that are 'good enough', rather than insisting on optimal solutions. Both are likely to facilitate the functioning of diplomats in multi-stakeholder diplomacy, helping them develop relations with a broad range of state and non-state contacts. The issue is whether their interlocutors are equally pragmatic and flexible or whether they will insist on optimal solutions, complicating the task of internet governance and the chances of securing any consensus, even at local level. In other words, will non-state actors in internet governance be socialised into behaving and thinking like diplomats, or will they serve as sources of uncertainty and volatility, complicating the regulatory process?

A final thought relates to the technologies of multi-stakeholder diplomacy and bottom-up regulation. In traditional, top-down regulation, what has been agreed is easy to establish. Government representatives meet and negotiate a single text of the regulatory framework. The normal principle is that nothing is agreed until all is agreed (for example, in the Brexit negotiations) and so the only document that matters is the last one. This is not true in bottom-up regulation, where the process consists of a series of agreements building up an ever greater body of regulatory norms. This allows considerable scope for disagreement over what has been agreed (possibly many iterations earlier) and for attempts to rewrite the history of the process. The blockchain technology that supports cryptocurrencies may be able to help here.[18] A blockchain essentially consists of a series of distributed registers in which transactions can be recorded in such a way that they cannot be altered. Thus an 'objective' account of all transactions can be recorded without a central authority and in such a way that the evidence continues to exist, allowing anyone to trace the history of all transactions back. Such technology obviously has attraction in a process of bottom-up regulation. Distributed registers could record the progressive agreements on internet governance in such a way that they could not be changed or falsified. The entire process of bottom-up agreements would be available to anyone who wanted to check it. Objectivity and reliability would be guaranteed without the need to create a central authority (or a new international organisation). One of the technologies that has generated the need for new regulatory frameworks would help in managing the challenges that those frameworks throw up.

4

Mitigating Cyberconflict

Cybersecurity is of growing concern to publics, as ever more cyberattacks are reported in the media. People are understandably concerned about the security of their data or the critical infrastructure on which modern life depends. The expanding Internet of Things, whereby a range of daily technologies are linked to the internet, increases both the sense of vulnerability and the range of possible targets ('attack vectors') for potential hackers. The term 'cybersecurity' is relevant to a range of different types of threats arising from different motivations (although often using indistinguishable methods). These include cyberwar, cyberespionage, cyberterrorism, cyber information war and cybercrime. In this chapter we will focus on the use of cyberspace in conflict between states (although, as we will see, non-state actors play a key role) and how diplomacy might mitigate its worst effects. We will examine cybercrime in the next chapter, when we will also look at companies as actors in cyberdiplomacy.

Before exploring in more detail the nature of conflict between states in cyberspace, it is worth reflecting a little on the relationship between diplomacy and conflict in physical space. As argued in chapter 2, the relationship between diplomacy and conflict is complex and not always contradictory. Diplomacy can be aimed at starting a war or improving the conditions under which a war can be launched. Once conflict has broken out, diplomacy can be aimed at ending it or at improving the prospects for victory by winning over neutrals or seducing allies away from the enemy. In physical space, statecraft (or grand strategy) consists in bringing together the full range of tools available, including diplomacy and warfare, but also other tools such as economic coercion, to achieve the state's policy objectives. A willingness to use military means will depend both on the issues at stake and on the political culture of the state concerned. If statecraft in the physical world sees diplomacy and warfare as two sides of a multisided strategic coin, then the same should be true of cyberspace. Whereas until now much of the focus in cybersecurity has been on the technical means to defend or attack (the equivalent of military solutions in physical space), little if any attention has been paid to diplomacy as a necessary complement of security approaches. This would be like conducting foreign policy with military tools only. The inevitable result would be increasing conflict and warfare (and probably a short life expectancy for the human race). The consequences in cyberspace may less catastrophic (for now at least), but, without introducing diplomacy in some way, conflict is likely to increase.

Cyberwar

Cyberwar is distinguished from other forms of conflict in cyberspace by the attempt to cause damage, whether to computer systems, to data or in the real world.[1] Thus a cyberattack might aim to degrade or prevent access to computer systems, corrupt data so that it can no longer be used, or damage computer systems in such a way as to cause death, injury or damage to critical infrastructure. This last is referred to as causing kinetic damage – for example, degrading the computer systems operating air traffic control so as to cause aircraft to crash. As we will see, one of the key questions is whether states can or should use kinetic attacks (causing damage in the physical world) to respond to non-kinetic attacks (causing damage only to computer systems or data storage). Cyberwar is carried out by states against other states, although states may use surrogates to carry out the attacks, either to conceal their role or because the surrogates have greater technical skill.

So far there has been only one clear-cut case of cyberwar, the Olympic Games attack against the Iranian nuclear programme.[2] The technical details of the attack don't concern us. It is assumed that the US and Israeli governments, in an attempt to delay Iran's development of a nuclear weapon, authorised a cyberattack against the Natanz nuclear materials processing plant. A worm (Stuxnet) was introduced to the computer systems operating key centrifuges, which sped them up and slowed them down beyond their specifications until they broke. At the same time the worm concealed what was happening from the Iranian engineers operating the centrifuges. It is not clear how effective this was in delaying Iran's nuclear weapons programme – the main effect may have been psychological. The attack was discovered when the virus escaped into broader cyberspace and was found on other computer systems. Although it appears to have done minimum damage, it does illustrate the danger of collateral damage from cyberattacks. In the case of the Stuxnet attack, the US and Israeli cyber experts appear to have identified a flaw in the software system operating the centrifuges which allowed them to enter and manipulate it before it was identified and fixed by the Iranians (such attacks are known as 'zero-day exploits').

A less clear-cut case of cyberwar occurred in the coordinated distributed denial of service (DDoS) attacks against Estonia in April 2007.[3] Estonia had decided to move a statue commemorating the Soviet army's role in the Second

World War to a less prominent position. Russian hackers responded by swamping key Estonian webpages with requests for information until the sites collapsed (and thus access was denied). All online services in Estonia were about to break down when the Estonian government thwarted the attacks by disconnecting Estonia from the rest of the world's internet. At first sight this would appear to be a case of a cyberwar attack aimed at degrading or denying access to computer systems. But the Russian government denied any involvement and blamed individual hackers outraged by Estonia's decision to move the statue. Although Estonia, and others, strongly suspected Russian government involvement, it could not be demonstrated in a relevant time frame. This illustrates a key problem with conflict in cyberspace: attribution, demonstrating conclusively (or at least to a sufficient level of certainty), and in a relevant time frame, who is responsible for a cyberattack (Florian Egloff has suggested an interesting parallel with privateers).[4] In the event, NATO allies came to Estonia's aid in helping to restore its online systems, but Estonia did not activate Article 5 of the NATO charter (the article that activates support from all other members of NATO to a member under attack), and the incident remains in the grey area between cybercrime and cyberwar. Russian cyberattacks on Georgia and Ukraine during the 2008 and 2014 wars fall more within cyber information war, which we will look at later.

Cyberespionage

Cyberespionage is the penetration of computer systems in other states in order to steal data. The data can be stolen for different reasons:

- to acquire intelligence on the intentions and capabilities of the government in question, either in cyberspace or in the physical world. Given the sheer number of penetrations of defence-related systems in the US or Europe (quite aside from those not reported), this would seem to be an almost continuous activity.

- to steal intellectual property, whether for the sake of stealing it, to increase the attacking government's own capabilities, or to pass it to its companies to increase their competitive advantage and reduce their expenditure on research and development. The Chinese seem to have been the main purloiners of intellectual property, although whether they had the capacity to take advantage of everything they stole is questionable.

- to prepare the ground for future cyberattacks, whether in the form of espionage or cyberwar. Penetrating foreign systems allows states to analyse weaknesses that could form the basis for future attacks, as well as leaving 'back doors' to guarantee gaining access to the systems in the future.

- to acquire sensitive or embarrassing information which can then be deployed in information warfare operations. This could simply be a case of demonstrating publicly the weakness of a government's key computer systems with a view to undermining the public's confidence in the government's ability to protect critical infrastructure (there may be a flavour of this in the theft by Chinese hackers of classified personal data about US government employers). This is the equivalent of 'pwnage', when one hacker demonstrates he has hacked another. Alternately, it may be more manipulative, as when Russian hackers penetrated the computer systems of the Democratic National Committee, stealing embarrassing emails which they then passed to WikiLeaks to release during the 2016 US presidential election.

As in cyberwar, the actual hackers may not have direct contact with their government. But for an activity to be cyberespionage, rather than just criminal theft of data, a government must stand behind it, directly or indirectly controlling the cyberspies.

Cyberterrorism

At various points over the last decade, public concern about the threat of cyberterrorism – that terrorists would use cyber tools to carry out some act of terror – outstripped concern about all other forms of cyberattack. The idea that terrorists would use the penetration of computer systems controlling critical infrastructures to produce a 9/11-type spectacular seemed all the more plausible as ISIS made a concerted effort to attract and recruit IT experts. However, so far this is the dog that has not barked. Terrorist groups[5] such as ISIS have undoubtedly made use of the internet, but mainly to recruit new members, carry out propaganda and steal money in online bank raids. These activities are of themselves of concern to Western security and intelligence agencies, but they do not amount to cyberterrorism. There are several reasons why we may not yet have seen cyberterrorism. Terrorist groups hanker after the visually spectacular – acts of atrocity which terrorise civilian populations.[6] Taking down a computer system or denying access to a webpage through a DDoS attack doesn't have the same impact. To produce an atrocity, terrorists would have to penetrate the computer systems controlling critical infrastructures such as air traffic control or energy supply. These systems are increasingly well protected, both at the external perimeter and on the inside. They can no longer be hacked by a lonely teenager from his bedroom. Terrorist groups may lack the resources, human, technical and financial, to take on such hardened targets (the Stuxnet attack took the combined resources of two of the most advanced cyber powers plus several years of preparation). By definition, terrorists look for soft targets. It may be simpler to plant a bomb or drive a car onto a pavement. This does not mean that the potential threat does not remain. As a shared danger, it could at some point provide a useful common ground around which to construct a diplomacy of cyberconflict.

Information Warfare

Cyberspace can be used to prosecute information warfare more effectively. There is nothing new about information warfare. The famous American diplomat George Kennan wrote a key State Department policy paper on what he called 'political warfare' as far back as 1948. But cyberspace opens up new possibilities for information warfare, in terms of both scope and reach. Cyber information war exploits online media outlets and social media to spread misinformation and disinformation to destabilise other countries' governments or undermine their political or economic processes. Russia currently seems to be the main protagonist of cyber information war (China appears, so far, to aim such activity mainly at its own population). Russia's invasions of Georgia in 2008 and the Ukraine in 2014 were accompanied by information warfare campaigns, seeking in particular to portray the Maidan protests as a Western-inspired coup and to equate the Ukrainian protesters with neo-Nazi nationalists. More recently there has been growing evidence of Russian cyber information war campaigns in 2016 to influence both the Brexit referendum and the US presidential election. We have seen above how, in the case of the latter, Russian hackers stole embarrassing emails from the Democratic National Committee, which they then passed to WikiLeaks to publish at a key moment in the election campaign. The US Justice Department has indicted twelve Russian military intelligence officers for their role in this. But so-called troll farms also deluged both the presidential and Brexit campaigns through Facebook and Twitter with misinformation, misleading stories or downright lies. It is still being debated whether these cyber information warfare campaigns in the end had any effect on the outcomes of the two votes.[7]

Interestingly, Russia refers to 'information warfare' (*informationaye protivorburstvo*) rather than 'cyberwarfare'. For the Russians, this includes electronic warfare, intelligence, hacker warfare and psychological warfare and is a necessary preparation for and accompaniment to conventional warfare.[8] This has led some Western observers to talk of hybrid warfare, conventional warfare combined with the use of insurgents, cyberattacks and information warfare – the so-called Gerasimov doctrine. In fact, the article in which Gerasimov articulates these ideas is a response to perceived Western hybrid warfare: he argues that the West combines economic support, democracy and human rights promotion campaigns and public diplomacy to overthrow pro-Russian regimes in Russia's near abroad, citing the colour revolutions and the Arab Spring.[9] Russia's adoption of hybrid warfare is a necessary response to the West's initiative. It is not necessary to debate the merits of Gerasimov's position, but it illustrates a further problem with cyberspace: that activities in cyberspace which some countries see as acceptable – for example, using digital tools and social media to enhance the effectiveness of public diplomacy campaigns – are seen by the other side as information warfare which must be countered.

Strategy in Cyberspace

Although it is reasonably straightforward to categorise the types of activity in conflict in cyberspace, it is harder to know exactly what, or how much of it, is going on. Countries do publish cybersecurity doctrines or strategies. Thus the US seeks 'global network dominance'. Russia focuses on the danger of 'the desire of a number of countries to dominate the global information domain'. China prioritises 'respecting and protecting sovereignty in cyberspace'.[10] But if countries are willing to adopt a formal public posture, they are understandably more coy about what penetrations they are perpetrating, or suffering. The whistle-blower Edward Snowden revealed extensive information about NSA surveillance operations, causing significant embarrassment for the US in the process, including with close allies (the NSA has lead responsibility for cyber operations). Much less is known about other types of operations, as victims are unlikely to speak out. There are a number of countries seeking to penetrate computer systems in other countries. Many rely on relatively unsophisticated means, depending on poor security practices to help them break passwords or persuade computer operators to open attachments containing viruses. Others with greater resources work on zero-day exploits, identifying and attacking flaws in software operating systems. Concerns are growing about upstream attacks, whereby hackers intervene in the fibre optics that carry internet traffic. As most internet traffic passes through the United States, US intelligence agencies have an inbuilt advantage that provokes suspicion in the rest of the world (even the EU is talking about a system to route its traffic through Schengen networks only). At the same time, the British have worried about the proximity of Russian submarines to transatlantic cables, warning of the dangers to the internet if they were to cut them (ironically, it was the British who cut the German transatlantic telegraph cables in the First World War, forcing them to send their classified traffic over British cables).[11] The number of states engaging in cyber operations is also increasing. For example, Iran responded to the Stuxnet attack by developing its own cyber capabilities, which it then used to attack the Saudi oil company Aramco.

There is a general consensus that, in the cyber arms race between the hacker and the cybersecurity expert, the hacker holds the advantage. While the experts strive to improve security against the last attack, the hacker is looking forward to the next one. Perimeter defences such as firewalls seem particularly vulnerable. In a twenty-first-century reflection of Stanley Baldwin's 1930s comment about bombers, 'the hacker always gets through' – well, often anyway. Zero-day exploits are by definition difficult to defend against. Even more difficult to manage is the everyday carelessness of computer operators who set weak passwords or open email attachments without confirming their provenance. When I was a junior diplomat I was shown a photograph of a safe with the combination number written in pencil on the wall next to it: the safe was in the British Embassy in Moscow during the Cold War. The equivalent today is to stick a post-it note with the password on the side of the computer screen. Given these difficulties, relying on perimeter security is rather like the French relying on the Maginot Line at the outbreak of the Second World War. The hackers, like the German army, just go round it. This has led to an increasing preference for developing measures that assume penetration of the perimeter defence. This includes creating sinkholes, which attract the attacker to a particular area of the system where he can be quarantined, and developing white worms that can disable hostile viruses. Most relevant for our purpose is that one of the most effective forms of cyberdefence may be cyberattack. Penetrating the computer systems of a rival may allow a government to identify that rival's capabilities and motivations. It may give a much clearer idea as to whether the rival is developing cyber capabilities with a view to an immediate attack or whether these are merely on a precautionary basis. If necessary, it puts a government in a position to take pre-emptive action. However, it can be hard for a foreign government to distinguish between a defensive penetration aimed at gathering intelligence about capabilities and intentions and an offensive penetration preparatory to launching a cyberattack. Indeed, there may not be any real difference between them, with the former quickly and easily turning into the latter.

The Cybersecurity Dilemma

Ben Buchanan[12] argues that this is one of the factors complicating what he calls the cybersecurity dilemma. In the classic security dilemma, state A is concerned about its security in relation to a more powerful state B. It therefore increases its military forces. State B, observing this, interprets A's military build-up as a hostile act and increases its own military spending. In the end, A has increased its military forces, but in doing so it has provoked an increase in military forces by B that leaves A worse off than it was in the beginning. The classic example is the Anglo-German naval arms race before the First World War. Germany was concerned by the implications of Britain's naval superiority for its growing overseas empire and therefore embarked on the construction of a high seas fleet that would allow it to guarantee access to its colonies. Britain interpreted the German naval build-up as a hostile move aimed at the British Empire and launched its own ship-building programme. By 1912 this naval arms race had finished in decisive victory for the British. The Germans ended up relatively worse off than they had been at the beginning and had alienated British public and political opinion in a way that would cost them dear two years later.

The security dilemma in cyberspace is potentially even more intractable. State A is concerned by the danger of cyberattack from State B and so develops further its cyber capabilities. State B interprets this as a hostile act and expands even further its cyber capabilities. The problem is that cyber capabilities are developed by being used. Unlike conventional weapons, cyber capabilities are not something you can store in a warehouse. If they are not being used, in a sense they do not exist. Rather like Berkeley's tree in the forest, if they are not being deployed in cyberspace, no one, including rivals, knows they exist. This leads to a reformulation of the cybersecurity dilemma: state A is concerned about a potential cyberattack by state B, so penetrates state B's systems to explore its capabilities and intentions. Rather than considering this as a defensive penetration, State B interprets it as an aggressive cyberattack and launches retaliatory penetrations of state A's systems. State A's efforts to improve its security have made its situation worse. But, if it didn't launch the defensive penetration of B's systems, would it leave itself open to a 'first strike' attack by state B? As Buchanan points out, the factors that can mitigate the security dilemma in physical space may not apply in cyberspace. For example, in the physical world, weapons systems can be positioned away from frontiers, signalling that their intention is defensive rather than offensive. Clearly such physical positioning is impossible in cyberspace. In the physical world, it may also be possible to distinguish between defensive and offensive weapons. For example, the purchase of fighter aircraft might signal less aggressive intentions than the purchase of bombers. But this distinction cannot be made in cyberspace. A penetration of computer systems for reasons of defensive espionage looks exactly like one preparatory to launching a cyberattack.[13] As we suggested above, one might swiftly change into the other, leaving the state whose systems have been penetrated little choice but to retaliate. This underlines the importance of accurate evaluation of intentions in cybersecurity.

Attribution

The issue of how to respond to cyberattacks, whether and how to retaliate, raises another series of problems. The first issue is attribution: how you identify the perpetrator of the attack and what level of certainty about attribution is necessary before taking retaliatory action. Although both Russia and China have governmental capacity for cyber operations (Units APT29 and APT28 of the Russian Federal Security Service (FSB) and Unit 61398 of the Chinese People's Liberation Army), they often prefer to operate through surrogates who, at least formally, have no connection to the government and who allow a degree of plausible deniability.[14] The FSB maintains a close relationship with organised crime – sometimes referred to as the *siloviki*–business symbiosis – and uses criminal hackers for government-inspired operations, for example the Russian Business Network or the online bank-robber Slavik,[15] who also appears to have gathered intelligence for the FSB. The troll farms which are used for information campaigns on social media in the West are ostensibly commercial companies. In China, so-called patriotic hackers 'spontaneously' launch cyberattacks in pursuit of China's interests (including intellectual property theft), while the 50 Cent Party (*Wumaodang*) provides bloggers ready to inundate Chinese social media with pro-government content. Western governments may be certain that the Russian or Chinese government is behind a particular attack or disinformation campaign, but generating sufficient proof to justify retaliatory measures can be difficult. Even if investigators can identify the servers from which an attack was launched, they cannot be sure that the real hackers have not hijacked these servers to conceal their identity and cast suspicion on others. The problem for policy-makers was shown in 'Cyber ShockWave', a televised simulation of a massive cyberattack on the United States conducted by the Bipartisan Policy Center with former senior government officials playing members of the National Security Council.[16] Despite being told the cyberattack appeared to have been launched from Russian servers, the participants were reluctant to attribute the attack to the Russian government and recommend retaliatory action. The techniques for investigating attacks and attributing responsibility are getting better but are still not perfect. Attribution may come, but is not always timely and does not necessarily carry the level of certainty that justifies retaliatory action. A 70 per cent certainty of attribution six months after an attack may not be a good basis for policy decisions. More-over, investigators themselves may not want to make public attributions, or the evidence for them, because of what it may reveal about their own investigative techniques and the extent to which they have penetrated other countries' computer systems. Americans knew immediately who had attacked Pearl Harbor. The culprit of a digital Pearl Harbor may not be so clear.

A Hobbesian World?

The unlikelihood of any rapid and effective retaliation makes a cyberattack seem a relatively low-risk option. Even if attribution is rapid and clear, unless the attack itself has been kinetic (caused physical damage or casualties), any retaliatory action is likely to be measured and proportion-ate. Unlike conventional weapons, cyberweapons cannot be stored away for a rainy day. A zero-day attack can only be carried out before the flaw in the operating system is discovered and patched. There is a sense of 'use it or lose it'. Combined, these factors lower the threshold for launching cyberattacks, whether aimed at doing harm or at gathering intelligence, in comparison to using conventional weapons. This in turn increases the risks of conflict in cyberspace. Indeed, it would be possible for a low-level conflict to be taking place in cyberspace without the public knowing. But there is also the risk of low-level conflict escalating into something more serious and spilling over into the physical world, either because of a rising escalation of retaliation or because the lack of retaliation encourages one party to overplay its hand. The difficulties of attribution and in dif-ferentiating between offensive and defensive penetrations may make the risks of geopolitical miscalculation greater in cyberspace than in the physical world. The danger is that, without the mitigating influence of diplomacy, cyberspace evolves into a Hobbesian anarchy of all at war with all. General Hayden, the former head of both the NSA and the CIA, has already said that there is no law in cyberspace.

In fact this is not quite true. Aside from the internet governance we looked at in the previous chapter, there have been various attempts to establish rules of the game for cyberspace conflict. In 2004 the UN General Assembly established the Group of Government Experts (GGE)[17] to consider cybersecurity issues. Its third report seemed to have secured a consensus that international law applied to all aspects of cyberspace, but Russia and China subsequently rowed back from this commitment. Its fourth report in 2015 agreed that states should not interfere with the ability of computer emergency response teams (CERTS) to respond to incidents, to support each other in investigating serious incidents, and to refrain from attacking or interfering with each other's critical infrastructure. But it was unable to agree to the prohibition of cyberespionage. This is understandable given that, in the physical world, the right of states to carry out espionage is tacitly accepted, including certain rules of the game (intelligence officers as opposed to spies are not usually targeted, espionage is not a *casus belli*, etc.). Given that the GGE was unable to agree a report in 2017, it is not clear if the process will continue in 2018. Various other more or less promising national, regional or even private-sector fora have been proposed for tackling the issue, although so far none have made real progress. China has proposed including cybersecurity on the agenda of the UN Conference on Disarmament. However, it is not clear what disarmament would mean in cyberspace, and the Conference on Disarmament itself is stalemated on other issues.

An alternative forum which has taken up cybersecurity has been the Council of Europe Convention on Cybercrime, otherwise known as the Budapest Convention.[18] Among other things (a major focus has been on child pornography and hate speech and racism), the Budapest Convention prohibits illegal access to systems and data, the interception of data, interference with data and systems, and intellectual property theft. These prohibitions are hedged about with provisions about government-approved activity (for example, government-approved interception or access to data), which rather undermines their effectiveness for governing interstate conflict in cyberspace. The Snowden revelations about the scope of NSA surveillance operations suggest that the United States, at least, has honoured the Budapest Convention more in the breach than in the observance. In any case, neither Russia nor China has ratified the convention, and both have made clear they have no intention of doing so (as too have India and Brazil), further limiting its relevance.

Another approach has been to try to apply the Law of Armed Conflict (LOAC)[19] to cyberspace. Derived from eighteen international treaties adopted over time, the LOAC can basically be divided into rules of behaviour during war (*jus in bello*) and the reasons that justify going to war in the first place (*jus ad bellum*). The *jus in bello* prohibits, for example, certain kinds of deception during war – false-flagging, disguising combatants as non-combatants, etc. It is difficult to see how this could make sense in cyberspace. The whole point of cyberwar is deception, penetrating other states' systems without their knowing. Nor is it clear how military systems in cyberspace could be clearly distinguished from civilian systems, especially as they are usually the same. Likewise, the LOAC lays down the rights and responsibilities of neutral states. But these assume clear sovereignty for the neutral state, which may not be violated, but nor may it support one of the belligerents. Again this makes no sense in cyberspace, where no such neutral territory can be marked out, and where a government has no idea about, or means of controlling, the data passing through fibre optic cables that may be crossing its country. The complex interconnectivity of the internet makes it hard to know what belongs to a neutral state and how to avoid damaging it in a cyberattack.

Similar problems lie with the *jus ad bellum*. The UN Charter lays down that a state may use violence against another only if authorised to do so by the Security Council by a Chapter 7 resolution or in self-defence (Article 51). The Tallinn Manual,[20] commissioned by NATO following the 2007 cyberattacks on Estonia, tries to establish what would constitute an armed attack in cyberspace under Article 51 of the Charter and what would be an appropriate response. The challenge becomes one of defining what constitutes an act of cyberwar. The manual distinguishes between cyberattacks that do not constitute a use of force, attacks that do constitute a use of force but do not constitute an armed attack, and attacks that amount to an armed attack. The distinction between the latter two categories appears to be one of scale. According to the manual, the cyberattacks on Estonia in 2007 did not constitute a use of force. The Stuxnet attack definitely constituted a use of force and may have amounted to an armed attack. The distinctions are important because they relate to the types of retaliation each permits. While insisting on proportionality, the Tallinn Manual opens the possibility of kinetic retaliation to cyberattacks that amount to a use of force or an armed attack. In other words, a state could respond to a cyberattack that has kinetic effects (e.g., damaging critical infrastructure) with a purely kinetic response (e.g., an air strike). Martin Libicki[21] convincingly argues that this increases the risk of escalation from cyberconflict to physical space conflict. If state A responds to a cyberattack by state B with a kinetic attack, this increases the risk of state B escalating to a higher level of kinetic attack. An alternative approach would be the Las Vegas rules, proposed by cybersecurity experts meeting in Las Vegas in 2016, by which what happens in cyberspace stays in cyberspace. In other words, any response to a cyberattack would be another cyberattack. This could undermine the power of deterrence against cyberattacks (state B might think more carefully about a cyberattack on state A if it thought the retaliation might take the form of a missile strike). But it would reduce the risk of conflict in cyberspace, where it might be more manageable, spilling over into physical space.

However, to be effective, any rules or norms of behaviour in cyberspace must be accepted by all the major players, including Russia and China. They will accept limitations on their behaviour in cyberspace only if the rules or norms benefit them too, above all increasing their own security. This is not impossible. Despite mutual mistrust in an existential struggle, much was agreed during the Cold War, including nuclear weapons reduction or restrictions (START I, the Nuclear Test Ban Treaty and the Anti-Ballistic Missile Treaty), as well as the tacit agreement that espionage was not a *casus belli*. Despite the conviction in both camps, especially among the military, that the other side could not be trusted and would cheat (some US military officials even feared that the Soviets would test nuclear missiles on the dark side of the moon to avoid the Test Ban Treaty), confidence-building measures were developed that allowed the treaties to be signed and, to a large extent, implemented. There is some evidence that such pragmatic agreements can be reached in cyberspace too. In September 2015, Presidents Obama and Xi Jinping reached agreement that China would curb online intellectual property theft from the US. Subsequently China reached similar agreements with other countries. The United States, fed up with the level of intellectual property theft by Chinese hackers, had indicted several individuals and threatened China with economic sanctions. It is not clear whether it was the threat of economic sanctions – which would outweigh the benefits China received from intellectual property theft (there is some evidence that Chinese hackers were stealing too much to process effectively) – that made Xi decide to cut the deal with Obama. It may have been a useful pretext for asserting his authority over China's somewhat anarchic cyber operations infrastructure. But in any event, so far, cyberattacks against the US from China aimed at stealing intellectual property seem to have fallen off dramatically.

Diplomats and Cyberconflict

Reverting again to the discussion of the nature of diplomacy in chapter 2, we can identify the key principles that would inform a diplomacy of conflict in cyberspace.

- There are no optimal solutions, only manageable outcomes. Good enough, even if flawed, is better than nothing – in cyberspace, a bad agreement is better than no agreement.
- Any international law or norms of behaviour we are able to establish for conflict in cyberspace are likely to function as they do in physical space. States will not use them as an absolute guide to behaviour but, rather, will be constrained by their wish to be seen to be obeying them, in their own eyes at least.
- Diplomatic communication is as important to minimise the risks of misunderstanding and misinterpretation in cyberspace as in physical space. Communication of intentions is particularly important in mitigating the cybersecurity dilemma. Marcus Holmes, basing his argument on recent advances in neuroscience and psychology, claims that frequent face-to-face contact is essential to successful assessment of intentions.[22] This suggests that old-fashioned face-to-face meetings, rather than digital communications, will remain essential to managing uncertainties and avoiding miscalculation in cyberspace.
- Without empathy, strategy is like playing chess with yourself. You always win, but it is poor preparation for playing with an opponent. Diplomats in cyberspace must be able to look at problems through the

eyes of rivals. In particular, diplomats must understand how those rivals see and interpret the actions and decisions of their own government and how that impacts the way they react and develop their own strategies.

- Professional diplomats will remain as essential in cyberspace as in physical space. Their socialisation in the international community of diplomats enables them to keep communicating and talking to each other when their political masters no longer can. As discussed above, this ability to maintain regular communication will remain essential to interpreting intentions correctly and to correcting any misinterpretations.
- Central to the diplomatic approach is the socialising of states into an international community of states and their representatives into an international community of diplomats in cyberspace. Given the importance of non-state actors and surrogates, we should aim, if at all possible, to socialise them too. But, given the nature of some of the surrogates used, especially, by Russia, that may not be possible. This should not necessarily worry us. Both sides in the Cold War were willing to use rogue surrogates against each other without damaging their ability to reach agreements (e.g., Soviet support for the Provisional IRA and other terrorist groups in Europe and US support for the mujahideen in Afghanistan).
- Public diplomacy is equally essential to diplomacy in cyberspace, especially in combating cyber information war and disinformation operations. Strategic communications campaigns, which seek to counter disinformation with 'true' information, are of limited value and tend to convince only those who already doubt the disinformation. This reinforcement of those who agree with us has psychological value but does little to reach those most vulnerable to

the disinformation or to convince them that the fake news they enjoy listening to is actually fake (we will revert to this in a discussion of algorithms later). More effective are public diplomacy campaigns, looking to build up trust and confidence over the longer term and willing to engage with genuine ambiguities (some of what we sometimes denounce as fake news can arise from genuinely divergent interpretations of geopolitical events; for example, did NATO promise not to expand into former Soviet republics in exchange for German reunification?).[23]

In order for a diplomatic approach to conflict in cyberspace to gain purchase, areas of possible common concern need to be identified where conversations might begin. Two possible themes might be cyberterrorism and avoiding anarchy in cyberspace. Although, as noted earlier, cyberterrorism is the dog that has not barked, there remains the risk of more sophisticated terrorists taking advantage of cyberspace in the future to attack critical infrastructures. All major states with cyber capabilities (with the possible exception of North Korea, but including Iran) have an interest in avoiding this. As the Internet of Things develops, all will become more vulnerable. One problem will be the definition of the term 'terrorist'. Countries such as China and Russia tend to use it more widely than other states to refer to internal dissent, violent or not. That may prove a barrier to a final agreement, but it should not prove a bar to initiating conversations. For similar reasons, the same states have an interest in preventing cyberspace becoming an anarchic Hobbesian world of all against all. In such a volatile and unpredictable cyberspace, no guarantees can be given over which state will be the one to suffer the catastrophic digital Pearl Harbor. Russia already seems to be suffering collateral damage from cyberattacks launched by the criminal friends of the *siloviki*.

There are two cautions that should be issued at this stage. Firstly, we should avoid, if at all possible, driving out or excluding states from the international community of cyberspace. Any such state would no longer feel constrained by the need to remain (or the hope of becoming) a member and so would not be limited by the necessity of obeying the norms and rules accepted by that community. The default setting for cyberdiplomacy is to attract and socialise states and representatives into the international community of cyberspace, not drive them out (however morally satisfying that may feel).

Secondly, we should beware Western exceptionalism. Western countries, especially but not exclusively the United States, are firmly convinced of their moral superiority. They believe that they can on occasion bypass the constraints of international law for the greater good: intervening on humanitarian grounds in Kosovo or Libya, declaring Kosovo's independence without UN cover, using drone strikes to assassinate Islamic terrorist leaders, ultimately invading Iraq to overthrow a cruel dictator. The intentions behind these actions may or may not have been morally admirable, and the frustration with the sloth and limitations of international law genuine, but the trouble is that they create an environment in which other states use Western disregard for the rules to justify their own exceptionalism, however cynically or with bad intentions. Thus Russia uses the application of the principle of self-determination to justify the seizure of Crimea, drone strikes to justify its assassination of its 'traitors' abroad, and support for pro-Western groups in Ukraine and pro-democracy and human rights groups in Russia to justify its interference in the US presidential and UK Brexit votes. Even the NATO-commissioned Tallinn Manual recognised that the Stuxnet attack was certainly a cyberattack that used force, and possibly an armed attack. So far it remains the nearest to a clear act of cyberwar we have seen. It has so far not provoked any similar attacks (although it did incite Iran to develop its own cyber capabilities, encouraging cyber proliferation), but it still risks being used as justification by another government in the future. If we want effective diplomatic management of cyberspace, and the possibility of norms of behaviour that will more or less function, we must be more willing to allow those norms to constrain us too, even when it is morally frustrating.

5

Business and Cyberdiplomacy

Companies and Geopolitical Risk

Companies increasingly participate in international relations as important non-state actors. To some extent this has always been the case for the major multinational companies. Not only did both the Dutch and the British East Indian Company act as sovereign entities in the seventeenth century, but more recently major oil companies have in effect created their own internal foreign ministries and pursued their own foreign policies, often separately from their national governments. But the process of globalisation, with the ever greater global interconnectedness it brings, especially in terms of information and trade flows, has meant that ever smaller companies are now international. Even companies that do not think themselves international are dependent on global supply chains that leave them vulnerable to foreign events, meaning that companies have a greater interest both in the impact of international affairs on their operations and, where possible, in finding ways of shaping that impact. They also have an interest in analysing and managing the geopolitical, political, economic and social risks to their financial bottom line. In other words, companies need to understand what kind of non-commercial factors could affect, positively or negatively, their international operations and how they might be able to mitigate the dangers (or take advantage of any opportunities).[1]

Cyberspace and the development of the Internet of Things reinforces this need for companies to focus on non-commercial factors and how they shape the international business environment in which they are operating. We have already noted that it makes little sense to distinguish between technology and non-technology companies. If globalisation means that all companies are international, the digital ecosystem in which we live means that all companies are tech companies. Even the little corner shop, dependent on global supply chains for the products it sells, depends on the internet to order those products, pay its taxes or manage its finances. This means that among the non-commercial factors that companies must understand and manage are the issues arising in cyberspace that we have looked at in the last two chapters. Companies must engage with cyberspace because it shapes their business models and decides if they are viable, and not only in terms of online competition. More specifically, companies must engage with cybersecurity, protecting their operations, data and customers, and participate in the regulatory debates about internet governance which will ultimately decide if their business models are viable.

There are three key questions about the engagement of companies and their executive with the geopolitical, or non-commercial, factors affecting their international and domestic operations, whether in physical space or cyberspace.

- Why do companies not just leave the analysis and management of non-commercial risk to their governments? After all, their governments have foreign ministries and diplomatic services specifically designed to analyse and manage geopolitical risk.

- Is there a specific diplomatic approach that businesses could adopt towards the analysis and management of geopolitical risk? This doesn't just mean businesses engaging with non-commercial issues, or even recruiting retired diplomats to their board, but acting in a way that could be described as diplomatic, which could amount to something called business diplomacy.
- Do businesses in fact already adopt an approach to these issues that could be called diplomatic, and, if not, would there be advantage in doing so?

Companies are subject to all the hazards described in the last chapter: cyberwar, cyberespionage, cyberterrorism and cyber information war. This should not surprise us. The same is true in physical space. Governments will attack the companies of foreign enemies for a variety of reasons. In warfare, foreign companies will be targeted by bombing to undermine the enemy's economic performance. Governments will spy on foreign companies, especially if those companies are major suppliers to the enemy's defence sector. Foreign companies, in particular their overseas offices, will be attacked by terrorists, who may seek to portray them as symbols of imperialist oppression (and they may also be softer targets – for example, the HSBC headquarters in Istanbul attacked by Islamic terrorists). Companies can even be caught up in information warfare, where misinformation is spread about their overseas (or domestic) activities in order to undermine the reputation or economic stability of their country. All of these translate into cyberspace. Iran responded to the Stuxnet attack on its nuclear programme with a cyberattack that took down the computing system of the Saudi oil company Aramco. Many of China's cyberattacks against the United States have been aimed not at the US government but at the private-sector Pentagon suppliers who hold much sensitive information about new American weapon designs.

Cybercrime

This chapter focuses on a further threat to companies in cyberspace: cybercrime. Cybercrime is distinguished from the other forms of cyberattack discussed in the last chapter by motivation and is aimed primarily at making money for its perpetrators. We will examine cybercrime not in the sense of dispensing illegal products or images (e.g., drugs or child pornography) on the internet but, rather, in the sense of cyberattacks against companies and their computer systems principally for financial gain. As we saw with the *siloviki*–criminal symbiosis in the last chapter, this distinction is not completely clear-cut. Cyber operations can serve both financial and political purposes at the same time.

The main kinds of criminal cyberattacks against companies include:[2]

- *data theft* – whether to steal intellectual property from the company or to steal the data of its employees, clients or suppliers;
- *financial theft* – the transfer of money from the company's accounts to the criminal's accounts, often via a series of intermediary accounts;
- *blackmail* – either by using data stolen from the company that could be embarrassing to the company or its clients (e.g., the theft of client data from and subsequent blackmail of the 'dating' site Ashley Madison) or through ransomware attacks (whereby the hacker freezes the victim's data until a ransom is paid, usually in a cryptocurrency);
- *damage to the company's computer systems* – which could be instigated by a rival or competitor to damage the company's operations or reputation or by an activist ('hactivist') with political complaints against the company.

It is difficult to put a value on the cost of cybercrime every year, as many companies, worried about their reputation with their clients or shareholders, do not publicise attacks. This is particularly true of ransomware attacks, where it is unclear how many victims pay the relatively moderate sum to secure the rapid restoration of their data. However, a report by the computer security company McAfee and the US Center for Strategic and International Studies[3] estimated that cybercrime is costing the global economy $600 billion annually, or around 0.8 per cent of GDP. This has been rising significantly over recent years and is set to rise further with the growth of the Internet of Things. One estimate puts the global cost of cybercrime by 2021 at $6 trillion. Already cybercrime is third – after government corruption and narcotics trafficking – in terms of its cost to global GDP.

Until now, companies have depended largely on technical perimeter defence against cyberattack. But this is no more effective for companies than it is for governments. At best it can be described as a necessary but not sufficient measure. Although none but the largest companies are likely to be specifically targeted by a zero-day exploit (zero days are far too valuable to employ in trivial attacks), any company may be a collateral victim of an attack exploiting a flaw in an operating system (for example, in the 2017 ransomware attack which took down, among others, Spain's main telecommunications company Telefónica). They are more likely to be penetrated as a result of careless practice among staff (not changing passwords or falling victim to a phishing attack) or the actions of a disaffected staff member. An additional problem for companies consists in their dependence on global supply chains. It makes sense in terms of efficiency to share information and even integrate systems. But it is not clear that supply chain partners operating in different cultures and different regulatory frameworks will necessarily take the same approach to cybersecurity. Even if the supply chain partners can be brought to common standards of security, it is not clear that these will be applied in turn to their local suppliers. Similar problems have been encountered with corporate and social responsibility (CSR). Even if supply chain partners can be persuaded to take CSR seriously, that may not be true of their local suppliers, whose activities might still damage the reputation of Western members of the supply chain.

Defensive Measures

Computer security consultants have responded to the weakness of perimeter defences by improving defences within computer systems for identifying and isolating viruses and intrusions. Like governments, companies can deploy honey pots or sinkholes to divert intrusions to places in the system where they can be isolated and quarantined. Even so, there is still a long way to go. According to another recent report, the mean time it takes for a company to identify a cyber penetration of its systems is 191 days, with a range between 24 and 546 days. Once identified, the mean time to contain a penetration is 66 days, with a range between 10 and 164 days. The mean time it takes to identify a malicious penetration (as opposed to one caused by human failure) is even higher, at 214 days.[4] These figures have improved because of the efforts of computer security consultants, but they still leave much to be desired. They are unlikely to engender confidence in the security of their data or online property among clients, suppliers or shareholders.

The vulnerabilities of companies to cyberattack raises the issue of whether they should be allowed to take proactive defensive measures – should companies be allowed to penetrate the computer systems of potential hackers to ascertain their capabilities and intentions, taking preemptive measures if necessary, even launching white worms to damage or destroy maleficent viruses? As we have seen, this kind of proactive defence already forms part of the cybersecurity armoury of governments. There are, however, several problems with allowing companies to take such measures. Firstly, very few companies have the technical and financial resources to carry out such 'defensive penetrations' or even the financial resources to recruit computer security consultants to do it for them. Allowing those that do have the resources to undertake this would be reinforcing their existing competitive advantage over rivals. Secondly, how would a company identify a potential hacker? What process of evidence and selection would be used? What would be the legal position if the company got it wrong or, even worse, damaged the computer systems of an innocent party? This raises the broader question of whether allowing companies to penetrate other computer systems as part of their cybersecurity measures is, or should be made, legal. In the physical world, commercial espionage by companies is illegal and the privilege of espionage against foreign governments is reserved to the government. Governments are likely to take the same view in cyberspace. The alternative would risk producing a chaotic entanglement of companies penetrating computer systems on grounds of cybersecurity in ways that governments would find hard to regulate.

The irony is that the very cyberspace that was supposed to undermine the power of governments may be making governments more relevant again. If the most effective form of cyberdefence is to penetrate the computer systems of potential hackers to ascertain their capabilities and intentions, and if only sovereign governments have the resources and the legitimacy to do this, then companies need to stick close to their governments. They must collaborate over cybersecurity, but, as with broader geopolitical risk management, cannot rely on governments to do it all for them. There may be a divergence of interests between the government and the company. While the company is focused on its own interests, the government has to take account of the interests of the country as a whole, and these may not coincide. Particularly where smaller countries are concerned, the government may not have the cyber resources or the diplomatic influence to help. Finally, as we will see later, the government may be part of the problem.

Diplomatic Approaches

If governments need to develop diplomacy to deal with cybersecurity, it is likely that companies also need to go beyond purely technical (especially perimeter) defences. As suggested, technical approaches are necessary, but they are not sufficient. Reverting again to the discussion in chapter 2, there are several ways in which a diplomatic approach could complement technical approaches.

- *Analysis of cyberthreats* There are technical approaches for trying to identify possible cyberthreats to companies, and possible hackers, that operate by 'scraping' information off social media and hacker chat rooms and then subjecting it to Big Data analysis (as we will see in chapter 6, Big Data analysis is problematic). A diplomatic approach to analysis would focus on the company itself, its operations, and the different markets in which it is operating. This analysis would be used to identify reasons, commercial and non-commercial, why the company might provoke cyberattacks and what type of hackers might attack the company.
- *Strategies for minimising attacks* Once a hacker has been identified, depending on their motivation, a diplomatic approach would use networks of influence and information to isolate him within his own community, discourage him from the attack, or even divert him against another target. Such methods are most effective against hackers with mixed political and financial motives and are less likely to be effective against those whose only motive is financial.

- *Diplomatic strategies for improving collaboration between governments and companies* Collaboration between companies and government and other companies is frequently less robust than it should be. A typical reaction of companies when one firm suffers a cyberattack is one of Schadenfreude, more relief at not having suffered themselves than a commitment to support the victim. The problem can be even more severe with governments, which are often divided against themselves on cybersecurity. While government departments officially want to enhance cybersecurity and protect their companies against attack, their intelligence agencies are focused on strengthening their ability to attack foreign computer systems when and as necessary, including exploiting zero-day attacks. While companies would prefer any flaws in operating systems to be communicated immediately to the software designers so that they can issue patches, intelligence services prefer to retain them for subsequent use, leaving the operating systems vulnerable (if a friendly intelligence service can identify a flaw in an operating system, potentially so can an unfriendly one). A diplomatic approach to these problems would first develop networks of influence and information among the key stakeholders, both governmental and non-governmental (including academic departments and the media, as well as other companies). Building on these networks, it would construct coalitions among these key stakeholders, both to improve coordination between companies and to ensure the right outcomes to government decisions.
- *Public diplomacy strategies to reinforce public support* Neither companies nor governments have been successful in garnering public support for cybersecurity. The public tend to blame companies for security breaches, complaining that they do not

take their responsibilities seriously. For many, the hacker is still seen as a lone, almost Robin Hood-like figure taking on the big corporations, rather than as a member of the criminal syndicate he really is. Most companies engage with the public on cyber-security only after they have been hacked, when it is too late and they are reduced to damage limitation mode. A diplomatic approach would involve a long-term engagement with the public, drawing on the full range of public and digital diplomacy pools. The aim would be to engage in a genuine dialogue about cybersecurity and the damage done by hackers, whether through conventional media, social media, conferences or other events, so that, when an attack takes place, public sympathy (the public of course includes key stakeholders such as customers, suppliers and employers) would incline towards the company as victim.

- *Socialise the supply chain* We have seen that a major problem for companies lies in the different attitudes and approaches towards cybersecurity from different members of the supply chain, often reflecting different cultures and regulatory frameworks. A diplomatic approach would seek to use public diplomacy along the supply chain to socialise the different members into a 'supply chain community', analogous to the international community of diplomats, with shared attitudes and ways of seeing the world and common approaches to cybersecurity.

There is another aspect of cybersecurity in companies that it is worth mentioning. Although, strictly, it does not come from a diplomatic approach to cybersecurity, it reflects the holistic and integrated manner to problems adopted by the diplomatic approach outlined in chapter 2. Most companies still see their core function as making money. They may accept other functions into the company, such as CSR, geopolitical risk management or cybersecurity, but these are seen as 'bolt-ons', not part of the core functioning of the company, and are confined to specialists in dedicated departments in headquarters. This approach may no longer be fit for purpose in the twenty-first century. It is particularly dangerous with cybersecurity. Creating centralised cybersecurity departments staffed by technicians charged with protecting the company against cyberattack encourages the idea that the responsibility lies only with those specialists. In fact, every employee is responsible for cybersecurity. It is highly unlikely that the computer experts will use weak passwords or open unverified attachments. Moreover, it is the ordinary employees who are most likely to spot a colleague who is careless with cybersecurity, or disaffected, or to identify local factors or vulnerabilities that could lead to a cyberattack. In the volatile and uncertain international business environment of today, cybersecurity needs to be integrated into the core of the company's functions (as indeed should be broader geopolitical risk analysis and management). This would also make more likely the effective deployment of the other diplomatic approaches outlined above.

Regulatory Debates

The second area in which a diplomatic approach could help companies is in their participation in the regulatory debates surrounding internet governance. If companies want to influence the current regulatory debates they must participate in them. This is equally, or even especially, true of the debates on internet governance. In a digital environment where all companies are in effect tech companies, the outcomes of these debates impact on the business models of all but the smallest companies. Even apparently abstruse and technical issues impact both on how companies operate and on their profit margins. All companies today hold data, whether from clients or suppliers – usually both. The debates on protecting data will impact on the uses to which such data can be put and how it can be stored. As we saw earlier, the EU has already taken a major step forward with the European General Data Protection Regulation (GDPR), which came into effect in May 2018.[5] This restricts the uses that can be made of the data of EU citizens, wherever it is stored in the world. Specifically, it prohibits any use, without the explicit permission of each citizen or organisation involved, other than for the specific purpose for which the data was collected or offered. This clearly has serious implications for social media and marketing companies. But every company holding data anywhere in the world will need to decide if it is going to identify whether that data originates with EU citizens, when it will have to apply the regulation, or whether it will be simpler and cheaper to apply the GDPR to all of its clients, effectively making EU law global law.

Practically all companies now use the internet, whether to advertise their products and services, sell these online, seek out suppliers, or communicate with clients, suppliers and governments. The speed at which their data is transmitted, and the priority it is given, matters to their business models, which means that the net neutrality debate matters as well. If telecommunications companies are allowed to treat different kinds of data differently, or charge extra for priority treatment, companies need to take this into account when designing their online strategies. More relevantly for our purposes, they need to decide where they want the debate to conclude and participate effectively in the networks of state and non-state actors through which these debates are being mediated. Even more obviously, it matters to companies how the debates on the regulation of the Over the Top are settled.[6] If companies are providers of OTT services, they will want to influence where and how they pay tax and who regulates their service provision or accessibility. If companies are in competition with OTT service providers, they will want to work towards different outcomes. But it is not enough just to lobby your local regulator in order to influence outcomes in a world of bottom-up regulation mediated through global networks of state and non-state actors. As we have seen with GDPR and net neutrality, the key decisions may be made in foreign countries thousands of miles away from the office of a company's official regulator.

As with cybersecurity, companies must work closely with their governments. But, once again, they cannot depend solely on their governments to manage this for them, and for similar reasons. Governments represent a whole range of issues, not all of which may reflect the interests of the company. In regulatory issues, governments are driven by political agendas influenced by public opinion, which can often be contrary to the interests of the company. In such cases the company needs to work first on public opinion, or, rather, the key non-state actors that are driving that public opinion, whether the media, NGOs or academics. Governments must also represent all the sectors in the economy, among whom there may be sharp regulatory disagreements. If a government is trying to promote its economy as a centre for internet innovation, it may be more sympathetic to the views of internet companies trying to preserve net neutrality than to the views of its telecommunications companies who argue that net neutrality results in internet companies getting an unfair share of the rewards. In such cases, telecommunications companies may prefer to work with foreign governments who take a different view of net neutrality, for example the US Federal Communications Commission. Indeed, this is a general point. In internet governance, companies should be aware of the positions of other governments and be willing to work with them when they share preferred outcomes. This is true whether their position on a particular issue aligns with their government or not. If it does, the company can support the government's efforts to build effective coalitions. If their own government does not share their preferred outcome, working with those that do can strengthen their hand in the regulatory debates.

Diplomacy and Regulation

If internet governance will be largely bottom-up and mediated through global networks of state and non-state actors, and if companies need to participate in these key regulatory debates to ensure outcomes that favour their business models (or, at the very least, to understand how they need to adapt their business models to the outcomes of the regulatory debates), how would the diplomatic approach support them in their endeavours? How would a diplomatic approach differ from more traditional business world means of lobbying or public relations? As with the diplomatic approach to cybersecurity, certain key aspects of the diplomatic approach to internet governance can be identified.

- *Analysis* The analysis must identify the key regulatory debates relevant to the company's business model as well as the key state and non-state actors who are participating in the debates. Non-state actors will include NGOs, user groups, the media and academics as well as other companies. As noted, among state actors may be governments or regulators in other countries and regional or international organisations. The analysis must understand both the preferred outcomes and motivations of the actors and the interrelationships between them. As ever in the diplomatic approach, empathy, the ability to see the issue (and ourselves) through the eyes of the other actors, is essential.
- *Network building* The company must build networks of information and influence among the key state and non-state actors identified during the analysis. These networks will form subsets of the

networks through which the regulatory debates are mediated. Building such networks is not straight-forward. Many of the non-state actors especially – competitor companies as well as NGOs – may be suspicious of the company's approaches. A company will need to deploy public and digital diplomacy techniques, working through the conventional media, social media and events such as conferences to establish contact with key stakeholders and build their confidence. To succeed, network building must involve genuine conversation and dialogue.

- *Coalition construction* Within the networks of information and influence, companies can begin to construct coalitions to press for the desired outcomes. To be effective, coalitions must be heterogeneous, bringing together a broad range of state and non-state actors. They will be built around shared pre-ferred outcomes rather than shared values or ideology. As the climate talks showed, such coalitions can create curious bedfellows. But managing such heterogeneous coalitions is not easy; it requires tact and integrity and a willingness to listen to the views and ideas of the other members of the coalition (skills we would commonly call diplomatic).

This diplomatic approach to participation in internet governance debates differs from other methods such as lobbying and public relations in several respects. Unlike lobbying, a diplomatic approach engages all the key stakeholders in dialogue over a long time period. Lobbying focuses on selling a message to a limited group of decision-makers, usually over a short time period, and is less likely to be effective in the more diffuse decision-making processes of bottom-up regulation (it is difficult to see how traditional lobbying would have worked in the climate change negotiations). Unlike public relations, the diplomatic approach seeks not only to improve the image of the company, or how others think about it, but to engage directly in the decision-making processes. Unlike both lobbying and public relations, the diplomatic approach recognises that the company is no longer a passive recipient who would like to influence those who take decisions but, rather, together with other non-state actors, an active participant in the decision-making process. The diplomatic approach also captures the sense in which business in the twenty-first century may be more about long-term engagement and working in partnership with others than competition in short-term zero-sum games. In some ways, the role of the company in internet governance can be seen as a mirror reflection of that of the government. In the 1990s, the branding consultant Wally Olins wrote that countries and companies were taking on each other's role.[7] The increasing global instability and security requirements, including in cyberspace, have meant that governments have reverted to behaving like governments. But at the present time it may be that companies need to behave more like governments.

There is one question from the beginning of this chapter left unanswered: whether companies have adopted the diplomatic approach to cyberspace and, if not, whether they would be better advised to do so. There is very limited evidence so far of most companies adopting the diplomatic approach to either cybersecurity or internet governance. Exceptions are the major internet companies Google, Facebook, Microsoft and YouTube which, in 2017, formed the Global Internet Forum to Counter Terrorism in order to combat extremist and terrorist content on social media.[8] The forum will focus on technical solutions for identifying and removing such content but will also explore research and partnership with governments and civic groups. In 2015, Facebook, Dropbox, Pinterest, Tumblr, Twitter and Yahoo set up the Threat Exchange,[9] a platform where companies could share information about common attacks. Microsoft has proposed a Digital Geneva Convention, which, among other things, would focus on internationally recognised criteria for attribution of cyberattacks.[10] Part of the reason for the difference in activism between internet companies and non-internet companies may be the pressure that the former feel themselves to be under from governments and public opinion to play an active role. But it may also reflect the extent to which most companies still do not see themselves as tech companies, and therefore consider both cybersecurity and internet governance to be areas where their role is essentially passive rather than being proactive protagonists. The attitude is outdated, if still prevalent. In cyberspace, all companies are tech companies, and all have an active interest in how the issues and problems that arise there are managed. The diplomatic approach can help them play an active and constructive role in protecting their (commercial) interests there.

6
Algorithms and Internet Companies

Diplomats need to challenge algorithms. Indeed, algorithms may prove one of the most significant challenges that diplomats will face in the next few years. But few diplomats, if any, seem to have noticed. An algorithm is a set of unambiguous instructions performed in a prescribed sequence to achieve a goal. Although the set of instructions must be finite, it can be highly complex, and difficult if not impossible for a non-expert to understand. Diplomats must confront the challenges posed by algorithms in two contexts: Big Data analytics and their use by internet companies in search engines and social media.[1]

Big Data

It has been argued that the analysis of Big Data, the massive quantities of data being generated both on- and offline, can make diplomacy more efficient, effective and inclusive.[2] It has been suggested that Big Data could be especially relevant to information gathering and reporting, understanding patterns in public discourse so as to tailor messages and measure the effectiveness of communication campaigns, and improving the provision of consular services. Big Data, by definition, overwhelms the capacity of human analysts to see and make use of helpful patterns or trends. Its sheer quantity and complexity of information requires non-human mechanisms of analysis and thus depends on algorithms to generate outcomes which human analysts and policy-makers can employ. The claim is that these algorithms can provide new information and challenge bias, improve government service delivery, and help policy-makers better understand people's perceptions and inclinations.

Because they are mathematical constructs expressed usually in apparently meaningless streams of algebra, algorithms give the analysts and policy-makers the impression of extreme objectivity and thus an exaggerated confidence in the outcomes. But the impression of objectivity is misleading.[3] The algorithms reflect the cognitive biases and epistemological prejudices of their designers. The identity, and education, of the designers becomes central to the assessment of the reliability of the algorithmic output. Given the complexity involved, the designers are likely to be mathematicians or technicians with limited, if any, understanding of the international affairs the algorithms they are designing are supposed to model. By the same token, the analysts and policy-makers who will use the output will be specialists in international affairs and foreign policy, with little if any understanding of how algorithms work. For them, the algorithms are merely black boxes that produce the Big Data analytics. As it is the application of mathematics to enormously large quantities of data, the output must be superior to that produced traditionally by human analysts. After all, if that were not the case, why would the foreign ministry have gone to the not inconsiderable initial expense of buying in the Big Data capability?

This is not just a theoretical concern. A similar problem arose in the financial sector. Within banks and investment houses, mathematicians and physicists designed highly complex models for analysing economic performance, and in particular the performance of the complicated and obscure financial products in which the banks and investment houses were investing.[4] Those designing these models, which were effectively algorithms, had little if any knowledge of economics or how financial systems operate. While the traders and senior executives in the banks and investment houses had a better understanding of economics and financial markets, they did not have the technical knowledge to understand the mathematical models. For them, these simply spewed out objective data about the performance of their investments, on the basis of which they made future investment decisions. Even those who may have had doubts about the validity of their investment strategies were largely silenced by the apparent objectivity of the analysis produced by the models. In the end this gulf in understanding between those who designed the models and those who used them was an important contributory factor in the 2008 financial crisis and the collapse of investment banks such as Lehman Brothers.[5]

Similar problems could arise in foreign policy-making. Far from challenging bias, the algorithms could create new analytical orthodoxies harder to challenge because of the apparent objectivity of the process. New forms of groupthink could be constructed far harder to challenge or break. In contrast to a human analyst, it is impossible to interrogate the output of an algorithm and question the bases of its judgement. Even interrogating the designer might not help, given the complexity of the process of interaction between the algorithm and the data. Some Big Data advocates argue that human analysts are still necessary, to give context to the algorithmic output. But it is not clear to what extent the human analyst would be able to challenge the Big Data analysis, or else policy-makers would perhaps put their faith in the human analyst rather than the supposedly objective algorithm. Ultimately it may be necessary to design algorithms to challenge, or red-team, the other algorithms, presumably designed by different technicians. At this point one is tempted to wonder whether the Big Data analytics are worth the candle. However, given their widespread adoption elsewhere, it seems inevitable that they are going to enter foreign ministries. Diplomats may need to think of ways in which human analysis remains primary, with Big Data analysis as a secondary system used to test and challenge the human analysts.

There is a further problem with the use of algorithms, especially for information gathering and analysis. The algorithms will, by definition, be connected to the internet, where the majority of the Big Data is being scraped. Even if a process could be devised whereby the information was collected separately from the analysis, and the analysis performed on computers not linked to the internet (creating what is called an 'air gap'), the Stuxnet case shows that such air gaps can now be jumped by intelligence services. The upshot is that the algorithm doing the analysis is vulnerable to being hacked by a rival or hostile intelligence service. Changing the parameters of the algorithm would allow foreign intelligence services to manipulate the policy decision-making of those dependent on its output. This amounts to another reason for foreign policy analysts and decision-makers to be sceptical of the outputs of Big Data analysis.

Social Media Algorithms

The second area where diplomats will have to face up to the challenges of algorithms is in social media or search engines. Social media companies appear to offer their platforms free to the public. In fact, of course, the public pay with their data (as the Facebook/Cambridge Analytica scandal has made clear).[6] Marketing is central to the business models of social media platforms. Social media companies develop algorithms that build up profiles of each user from the data that he or she shares online. These profiles enable the companies to target each individual with adverts for products or services in which they will be interested. The aim is that each user only receives adverts they are likely to find interesting. But the same algorithms also govern the news, opinions and friends that social media offer their users. In each case, the algorithm ensures that each user is only offered what they are likely to like or agree with. Concern has already been growing about the way in which society is being fragmented into echo chambers where people listen only to the news or opinions with which they already concur, and their prejudices are thereby reinforced. The algorithms driving social media strengthen this trend, all the more so as ever more people rely on social media for their news. A recent Pew study estimated that over 70 per cent of American adults now get at least some of their news from social media, with 20 per cent doing so regularly.[7]

A similar problem arises with search engines. The results they produce are not randomly ordered, but nor are they objectively ordered in terms of relevance to the search question. Some results receive high priority because their 'owners' have paid for their webpages to appear at the top of the search results. In as far as it is always clear that these are paid advertisements or promotions, this is not important. Users know what they are getting. The order of the other search results is decided by the algorithms driving the search engine. Because users do not know how these algorithms function, and may even assume a random or objective production of search results, their search for information can be manipulated. The algorithms may focus on their previous search history, in which case they are constantly receiving similar responses, reinforcing existing prejudices or biases. Alternatively, the algorithms may function on some other principles, which can be studied by those who want to influence the ordering of the search results, perhaps to give their webpages priority without paying for it. There are a series of techniques known as search engine optimisation (SEO) which claim to maximise the internet traffic passing through a webpage through referrals from search engines or social media platforms. Sometimes the results can be malign. If anyone searched via Google in 2015 for how many people died in the Holocaust, the first four or five webpages listed were by Holocaust denial groups questioning how many, if any, had died. Neo-Nazi groups had 'gamed' Google's algorithm, using SEO techniques to ensure that their pages came out first. In this case Google was culpably slow in putting matters right.[8]

The use of algorithms in social media and search engines poses serious challenges for diplomats, especially those engaged in public diplomacy.[9] Their impact in reinforcing echo chambers and the fragmentation of social and political debate makes it much harder for diplomats to engage with foreign publics as a whole. To do so, they have to engage with each echo chamber separately, targeting their messages accordingly. But this risks fragmenting the coherence of their own public diplomacy, and ultimately their foreign policy. To the extent that public diplomacy increasingly depends on social media, the algorithms involved pose another problem. If the algorithms ensure that users receive only news and opinions which they will like (reinforcing prejudices), this means that diplomats using social media for public diplomacy will reach only those who already agree with them. While there may be value in reinforcing the views of those who agree with us, public diplomacy must surely attempt to convince those whose views are different. The whole aim of public diplomacy is to influence foreign public opinion so that it will, in turn, influence the decisions that foreign governments take. But this is difficult if, thanks to social media algorithms, you cannot even reach those who disagree with you.

Search engine algorithms pose different challenges for diplomats. Firstly, diplomats will want to ensure that their own websites and data get favourable treatment, with the maximum possible traffic being referred to their webpages, whether embassy or government, from search engines and social media platforms. This means that diplomats need to learn SEO techniques and apply them in webpage design, but also in the drafting of webpage content and key speeches by ministers and senior officials. But they also need to be aware of the danger of hostile or rival powers manipulating search engine algorithms to ensure that searches do not produce damaging, misleading or plain dishonest results. This implies constant monitoring and testing key questions, including in the local languages where they are serving. If, in the old days, the first job of a political officer in an embassy used to be monitoring the local media, in the twenty-first century it may be checking the search engines. In a sense, this becomes the diplomatic equivalent of searching your own name in Google.

In fact, the situation generated by algorithms is much worse. Echo chambers and the fragmentation of political social debate are not a problem for information warfare practitioners but, rather, an opportunity. Their objective is not to engage with foreign public opinion as a whole in order to influence their governments. On the contrary, their aim is to reinforce the echo chambers and further fragment social and political debate so that they can undermine unified government narratives. They are not concerned about relaying coherent messages as they are never going to admit publicly to the messages they are putting out. They will operate always through surrogates, whether supposedly independent media companies or troll farms. Messages can therefore be designed to reach each of the different echo chambers, and the algorithms in social media will ensure they reach their targets. The governments, or organisations such as the EU and NATO, who respond by reinforcing strategic communication are missing the point. The information warfare tactics combined with social media algorithms mean that people are getting the misinformation ('fake news') that they are already predisposed to believe. They are accordingly likely to reject government strategic communication as propaganda. The same social media algorithms, of course, mean that strategic communications are likely to get only as far as those who already agree with the government.[10]

There are two consequences of this. The first is that public diplomacy, seen as long-term engagement in genuine conversations and dialogue, is likely to be more effective in countering information warfare than strategic communication. This will be unwelcome to policy-makers, as public diplomacy takes time to produce results and consumes far more resources than strategic communication,[11] especially if it has to get round social media algorithms by largely eschewing digital tools. But, confronted by determined and well-constructed information warfare campaigns, the alternatives to investing in public diplomacy are ineffective strategic communication or responding with similar information warfare campaigns. The second is that diplomats need to take internet companies seriously as international relations players in a category all of their own. This is a question not simply of engaging with companies as non-state actors in regulatory debates (as discussed in the previous chapter) but also of recognising that such powerful companies are able to shape the international environment in ways that affect how interstate relations take place, and that they must accept the responsibilities that accompany this power.

Engaging with Internet Companies

In 2017 Denmark appointed the first ambassador to the tech sector[12] (France has quickly followed suit). His focus is on developing relations with the major internet companies in the same way as a traditional ambassador would with the country to which he is accredited (although the Danish ambassador has pointed out the major difference that he does not wear a suit or tie). The major objectives of this innovative Danish initiative appear to be:

- to engage with technology companies to discuss the implications of the new technologies, both for diplomacy and international relations, and more broadly for Danish society;
- to collaborate with the internet companies on ethical and political issues such as data protection;
- to attract technology and internet companies to Denmark and ensure that the country remains at the cutting edge of new technologies;
- to establish and reinforce Denmark's international reputation at the forefront of innovation in both diplomacy and technology.

In many ways this looks a very traditional agenda for a bilateral embassy, though translated into the technological preoccupations of the twenty-first century. This embassy must discuss the implications of policy decisions by the country to which it is accredited (the virtual country of technology and internet companies), collaborate with it on finding solutions to global regulatory issues, promote its inward investment in the home country, and develop public diplomacy strategies to enhance the reputation of the home country. But the evolution of information warfare, and the role of internet companies, may require an even more traditionally geopolitical role whereby the technology and internet companies are treated as potentially difficult state actors, albeit very authoritarian ones. Countering information warfare will require a far deeper understanding of the social media and search engine algorithms being taken advantage of by information warfare practitioners. Such companies as Facebook, Twitter or Google will be very reluctant to share this information. Their business models depend on the marketing revenues generated by their algorithms, the design and structure of which are what give them their competitive advantage over rivals. It is the most confidential and highly protected information these companies possess. Their main concern in sharing this with government is that it might leak to rival companies, or that government intelligence or security agencies may thereby take advantage for infiltration or manipulation.

Asking these social media platforms and search engines to share their algorithms is like asking a foreign country to share its most sensitive military secrets. Diplomats will need to convince them that it is in the common interest. But even this may not be enough. They may need also to paint a convincing picture of the dire consequences of not collaborating. Like any diplomat creating a strategy to secure the collaboration of a reluctant state actor, they will need to build coalitions of like-minded and state and non-state actors to apply pressure, as well as develop a convincing narrative. In this case they can take advantage of the public's growing disillusion with the internet companies, albeit over misuse of personal data, especially after the Facebook/ Cambridge Analytica scandal. But they may also need to develop a narrative where the West responds to the use of search engines and social media for information warfare with its own counter information warfare. The internet companies would have to decide if they would want their social media platforms and search engines reduced to the battlefield for a twenty-first-century information war. No doubt they would reflect on the impact this might have on their advertising revenues when deciding whether collaboration was the lesser of two evils. It is no coincidence that these are the same kinds of arguments that diplomats might deploy in seeking to persuade a state to rein back its information warfare campaign: 'Do you really want us to turn the same kind of information warfare against you?' Sometimes diplomacy in cyberspace feels awfully like the more traditional kind of diplomacy in the physical world.

7

Conclusion: Building Diplomacy Online

The central theme of this book has been the application of diplomacy to the problems arising in cyberspace. In many ways the nature and structure of the problems in cyberspace mirror those in physical space, and the distinction between the internet governance and cybersecurity agendas mirrors the distinction between the global issues and geopolitical agendas in the physical world. Just as more traditional geopolitical agendas threaten to distract governments from the global issues agenda and undermine efforts to resolve its problems, so cybersecurity issues threaten internet governance. In both physical space and cyberspace a broad range of state and non-state actors are now active participants in international affairs, offering different, and sometimes conflicting, visions of how problems might be resolved. In some cases both state and non-state actors can be the problem as well as part of the solution. As the hegemony of the United States declines and divergent views of global governance emerge, the rule sets governing international political and economic relations fragment. Western-inspired value systems are contested. International organisations stagnate and the prospects of creating new international institutions diminish. States and regional organisations respond to the fragmentation of rule sets by leveraging their economic power of attraction to impose extra-territorial legislation, whether it be the US imposing the Foreign Corrupt Practices Act in physical space or the EU the GDPR in cyberspace. The impact of this transition towards a multipolar world is felt as much in cyberspace – where it is encapsulated by the disagreements between the free internet countries and the cyber sovereignty advocates – as in the physical world.

Constructing twenty-first-century international governance, whether in cyberspace or physical space, will need to take account of these changes. Rather than intergovernmental agreements leading to new international organisations which impose top-down regulatory frameworks, new governance in both the physical world and cyberspace is more likely to be constructed bottom-up through networked debates between the full range of state and non-state actors. These regulatory debates will themselves take part in both arenas. The model is likely to be the networked debates of state and non-state actors that led ultimately to the Paris Agreement on climate change, with heterogeneous coalitions forming around shared preferred outcomes. Key new regulatory debates are likely to centre on new technologies such as artificial intelligence, machine learning and genetic manipulation, and acceptable and unacceptable applications of these. The multi-stakeholder diplomacy required will be the same as for internet governance. Dividing internet governance off from these other regulatory debates would not only make little sense, it could miss trade-offs between different regulatory domains.

Digital technologies took diplomats by surprise. To a large extent diplomats have still not caught up and struggle to develop a role in cyberspace. It is worth considering, therefore, what is coming down the road and what it might mean both for the tasks they should carry out and how these should be carried out. Most immediately, fifth-generation (5G) mobile telephony is due to be rolled out over the next few years and will massively increase connectivity and the quantity and speed of data over mobile networks. This could finally realise the vision of the mobile diplomat linked by built-in devices to regional hub embassies and her ministry, streaming information in real time and participating in policy debates while on the move. The security will be reinforced by end-to-end encryption.[1] But there are also geopolitical implications. The second phase of 5G will focus on connectivity between devices rather than people, enhancing the development of the Internet of Things. China, in particular the telecommunications company Huawei, has been focusing on developing the technologies for the second phase of 5G. It is possible that, for the first time, the key technologies facilitating a digital network, and thus the protocols for its operation, will have been developed in China rather than in the US, in a country that is a cyber sovereignty advocate rather than a free internet nation. This will have implications not only for how 5G operates but also for wider internet governance debates.[2]

The major development in the next few years is likely to be the combination of artificial intelligence (AI) with digital networks. Although artificial general intelligence (AGI) may be some way off (twenty to fifty years according to the expert consulted), machine learning is allowing computers and robots to excel over humans in specific tasks or games (e.g., chess or Go). By combining neural networks, powerful computers and enormous quantities of data, computers and robots 'teach themselves' to perform certain tasks (this is how the Alphago program beat the world Go champion). A key question here is how much autonomy in decision-making we are willing to allow to machines for different tasks. Are we going to insist that humans remain inside the decision-making process (in-the-loop or automated systems) where the human takes the key decisions while the machine automates implementation? Are we willing to allow the machine to take the key decisions itself based on the data and its algorithms, yet retain a human with a veto over the final choice to act (on-the-loop or semi-autonomous systems)? Or are there certain functions where we are willing to allow the machine to take decisions entirely autonomously without any human intervention (out-the-loop or autonomous systems)?[3] Much will depend on the tasks involved and the perceived risks of machines going rogue.

So far this debate has been fiercest over the possible use of autonomous machines or robots operating in warfare. There are already many automated and semi-autonomous weapons systems deployed. For example, the Aegis Ballistic Missile Defence System (ABMD) can operate in both automated and semi-autonomous mode. In the former, a human operator identifies the target and instructs the ABMD to fire. The automated systems ensure that the missile destroys the incoming target. In semi-autonomous mode, the system automatically identifies the target and will fire unless the human operator vetoes the launch.[4] The real debate centres on what are called LAWS (lethal autonomous weapons systems), systems that, once deployed in a battlefield or conflict zone, would take decisions on what to attack (and kill) based on algorithms and data, without human intervention. It is not clear that any such weapons yet exist (the Israeli anti-radar missile system Harpy may be the closest to a LAWS so far deployed). While the UN has created a Group of Government Experts to discuss the issue,[5] so far discussions have made little progress beyond identifying the challenges and better understanding the key issues. Although some experts, especially in the non-governmental sector, maintain that LAWS should be banned, this may prove unrealistic, especially if their possession delivers significant strategic or tactical advantage. Discussion is likely to focus on what kinds of systems might be permitted and the circumstances in which they might be deployed. Equally important will be their implications for international humanitarian law and the Law of Armed Conflict. For reasons mentioned earlier, these deliberations are unlikely to work if limited only to governments and international organisations. As with the landmine ban, governments will have to work together with companies (especially internet and technology companies), NGOs, academics and civil society groups. Diplomats and foreign ministries will again be required to demonstrate a capacity for multi-stakeholder diplomacy and for mastering the technical issues involved.

But AI and machine learning are not just generating new issues for diplomats to manage. They also have implications for diplomacy itself. While it may be too early to talk of PADS (peaceful autonomous diplomatic systems) or diplobots, many aspects of diplomacy are already being automated, or on the way to being so (e.g., visa applications, embassy security, some consular work). The combination of autonomous drones with digital communications (especially with the roll-out of 5G) will allow foreign ministries to monitor conflict zones that would be too dangerous for the presence of human diplomats (as one of the embassy observers on Tiananmen Square on the night of 3–4 June 1989, I write with some feeling about this). Diplomats and citizens need to debate now what kinds of diplomatic functions can, or should, be automated, and whether there are any diplomatic functions that might eventually be performed by fully autonomous machines, with humans left out of the loop. These are not straightforward issues. Although most of us rebel instinctively against the idea of LAWS taking decisions about destroying targets or killing people, some experts argue that they could render warfare more humane by reducing collateral damage and 'heat of battle' killing. Likewise it is conceivable that machine learning devices could be developed for negotiating which would autonomously identify the optimal outcome for both sides, without the interference of emotion or other 'human' factors. In practice this would probably be a 'human-on-the-loop' system, in as far as the government could still reject the outcome proposed by its diplobots (as they often do the recommendations of human negotiators). However, Holmes's work on the neurobiology of intention identification,[6] as well as that by Wheeler on building trust between former enemies,[7] suggests the need for human diplomats in frequent physical contact will remain important. The international community of diplomats will still be needed.

Machine learning may impact on the practice of diplomacy in a more immediate way. We have already looked at the potential drawbacks of Big Data as part of foreign policy analysis, and in particular its dependence on algorithms little understood by policy-makers. But at least these algorithms are designed by human engineers, who can be interrogated about the epistemological biases and presuppositions behind the algorithm design (even if this is not done as often as it should be). Someone understands how the algorithm works, even if they do not necessarily understand the policy issues depending on the algorithm's output. But this is changing. The next generation of Big Data algorithms is driven by machine learning. Neural networks are fed massive quantities of data, from which they then develop their own algorithms (again, essentially the approach Alphago used to learn how to play Go). At first sight, this should remove the epistemological bias of the designer. However, it remains in a more subtle form. Bias now depends on the selection and quantity of data fed to the neural networks to 'train' them into developing the algorithm. More concerning is that now not even the computer engineers understand how the neural networks have developed the algorithms. They have 'done it on their own'. This is truly a black box, where there is no one to interrogate about the way in which the data is analysed or how that impacts on the output. It again emphasises the importance of keeping humans in the geopolitical analysis loop.

The diplomatic approach to cyberspace identified in this book builds on the idea of an international community of diplomats and the process of socialising international actors within that community. In today's context, the idea is to construct an international community of diplomats within cyberspace. A key question for the twenty-first century, as much in cyberspace as in physical space, is whether the new non-state actors will become socialised within the community of diplomats and, if they do not, what it would mean for the prospects of international governance and stability. Would the increasing role of NGOs, who see the world in black and white terms and who insist on holding out for optimal solutions, make it harder to negotiate minimal governance agreements? Would the growing role of companies and business executives lead to an excessive focus on economic factors? In short, does the increasing multiplicity of non-state actors make internet governance easier or harder to achieve? There are other socialisation processes at work here as well. It is not just a question of whether diplomats socialise non-state actors into thinking and acting like diplomats. Diplomats too can be socialised, for example by NGOs, to begin thinking and acting more like civil society actors. This can be seen when diplomats start prioritising expressions of moral outrage over formulating effective foreign policy or cold-shouldering the diplomats from those countries they disapprove of. Diplomats can also be socialised by business executives into prioritising commercial promotion over geopolitics, evident in the way in which foreign ministries have sought to justify their budgets since the economic crisis in terms of their role in promoting business abroad. Other roles, such as political reporting and networking, have been downgraded. This is ironic at a time when political and geopolitical events increasingly impact on the financial performance of the companies foreign ministries claim to promote, in both cyberspace and physical space.

This book has discussed the limitations of social media in public diplomacy and, in particular, the problems of algorithms and the way in which they restrict who can be reached by diplomats. In general these algorithms will mean that messages will only arrive with those who already agree with the message. Information warfare can take advantage of this by tailoring multiple messages to reach multiple echo chambers. But the objectives of information warfare are essentially negative, seeking to cause confusion and uncertainty rather than trying to get across a coherent message or series of messages. Unless diplomats want to respond to cyber information warfare with counter cyber information warfare, bringing about an escalation which will only increase uncertainty and instability and reduce social media platforms to information warfare battlegrounds, they need to become more innovative (and less lazy) in their use of online tools. Rather than relying on off-the-shelf tools, where others write the algorithms, they need to develop tailor-made tools. Using online platforms to host scenario-building or simulation exercises helps diplomats escape the tyranny of the algorithms. Such exercises can be used to help build consensus in internet governance, resolve or minimise conflicts, and illustrate the benefits or dangers of following certain paths in ways that can engage the broad range of state and non-state actors. Gamification – using computer games as educational or marketing tools – may prove a more effective way of reaching out to and influencing younger generations than tweeting. Computer games can, of course, incorporate simulation or scenario-building exercises and can become networking tools in their own right. Innovation in the design and use of online tools and platforms will be essential to multi-stakeholder diplomacy.

At the moment, most diplomats are 'green-card holders' in the digital world (in Stanley McChrystal's felicitous phrase).[8] But gradually they are being replaced by digital citizens who have grown up in the digital world and are accustomed to living and interacting online and comfortable with digital technologies. One can only speculate how this will change diplomacy as they rise to positions of power. President Trump's habit of tweeting at all hours has already proved traumatic for diplomats, both US and foreign. But one can imagine a future generation of politicians and diplomats using online platforms for simulation and scenario-building exercises before taking decisions. If a suitable, and credible, neutral platform could be established, countries could use it to 'game' conflict situations before committing to potentially dangerous policy decisions (one can imagine what might have happened had political leaders in July 1914 been able to game the Balkan crisis, especially if they had all been participating in the same game; had they been able to test the possible outcomes in an online simulation, would they still have gone to war?). Would the digital UN of the future be able to provide an online platform which would be regarded as sufficiently credibly neutral by its members?

Diplomats must also start engaging more effectively with the major internet companies. This is not a case of just engaging with another commercial company. The major internet companies do not only provide services or platforms for their clients, they also shape cyberspace and how it functions. The algorithms that drive their platforms and search engines facilitate the spread of misinformation and information warfare while complicating and undermining efforts to combat them. The internet companies themselves need to understand better how they function in cyberspace and accept their responsibilities. Diplomats need to treat them as major powers, and not always friendly or cooperative ones. The Danish idea of an ambassador to the tech sector is a good one, but the remit must include pressuring the internet companies and, if necessary, spelling out to them the consequences for their own business models of not collaborating more fully in internet governance and combating information warfare.

The central role of the state is to protect the security of its territory and its citizens. The exaggerated decline of the relevance of the state was put in context in physical space by 9/11 and its subsequent centrality in protecting its citizens against international terrorism. Similarly, in cyberspace, despite the plethora of non-state actors and their importance, the cybersecurity agenda ensures the continued relevance and importance of the state. Only states, or state-backed groups, have the technical and financial resources to penetrate well-protected targets or to defend critical infrastructure against cyberattack. Only states have the legitimacy to penetrate foreign computer systems to ascertain capabilities and motivations. But, as the discussion of the cybersecurity dilemma showed, understanding the intentions of other states remains a major problem for cybersecurity. Cyberweapons cannot clearly be differentiated between offensive and defensive, nor can they be positioned defensively away from borders. A defensive penetration of another state's computer systems to ascertain capabilities and motivations can look the same as an offensive penetration in preparation for a major cyberattack. Effective evaluation of intentions and the ability to understand the interpretation of one's own actions become essential to avoiding ever escalating cyberconflict. Holmes's work on the neurobiology and psychology of face-to-face meetings, and the importance of regular face-to-face encounters to the correct understanding of intentions and the development of empathy, suggests the importance to cyberspace of diplomats in physical space in regular contact with each other. Although digital tools can enhance and facilitate some aspects of the diplomat's work, they may be of limited value in the evaluation of intentions.[9]

The problem of evaluating intentions, combined with the difficulties in attributing cyberattacks, the likelihood of limited damage from retaliatory attacks, and the perception of limited kinetic collateral effects (which may be an illusion, as the escape of the Stuxnet virus into the wider internet showed) may lower the threshold for cyberwar. In an international system with increasing tensions, but where nuclear weapons limit the options for major interstate warfare, cyberwar may seem a low-risk option. The danger of international tensions resulting in more or less permanent cyberwarfare is not negligible. In contrast to physical space, where warfare is hedged round by the Law of Armed Conflict (which most states at least make a pretence of obeying), in cyberwar there are at present few if any agreed norms of behaviour. It is not clear what status even the modest agreements of the Group of Government Experts enjoy (e.g., not to attack critical infrastructure). Even such a key issue as to whether a state can respond to a cyberattack with kinetic retaliation remains unsettled. In as far as the US has retaliated against Russian cyber information warfare (and threatened to retaliate against Chinese cyberespionage) with economic sanctions and the expulsion of diplomats, it appears that what happens in cyberspace does not stay in cyberspace. But responding to a cyberattack, even one with significant kinetic damage, with a missile strike would be qualitatively different and open the prospect of cyberconflict escalating into physical world warfare.

The diplomatic approach to establishing norms for cyber-conflict would begin with the construction of an international community in cyberspace, to which the majority of state and non-state actors would want to belong, and then move to the development of a body of norms that members of that international community would be expected to obey. It would accept that, as in physical space, international law is largely self-policed. Actors constrain their behaviour so as to appear (at least to themselves) to comply with international norms. This implies a certain modesty in objectives. In the diplomatic approach, it is more important to maintain the various actors within the international community than to insist on strict compliance with all the norms. As long as actors believe themselves within the international community, their desire to remain so will serve as a restraint on their behaviour. Once they consider themselves to be outside the international community, they will feel no such restraint. The diplomatic approach would also accept that the norms of the international community in cyberspace will not neces-sarily reflect Western values or preferences. If the conclusion is that some kind of order in cyberspace is better than no order, and some kind of constraint on behaviour is better than Hobbesian anarchy, then Western countries may have to compromise to get cyber sovereignty advocates on board. Maintaining a functioning international community is not easy and demands constant management. Bad behaviour by members of that community can provoke understandable moral outrage in the media and among publics and politicians. This makes the role of diplomats, who can maintain the conversations and the relationships which retain at least the possibility of a continuing international community, all the more important, and it reinforces the need to avoid diplomats being socialised into civic society activists or business executives. Being a diplomat may not appear ethically attractive or heroic, but it is heroically unheroic, insisting on the unfashionable virtues of moderation and compromise. The diplomatic role remains as essential to cyberspace as it does to physical space.

There is no need to start from scratch. There is already an international community of diplomats in physical space, as there is an international community of states. With multiple crises and disagreements between the West and countries such as Russia, Iran and Syria, and with non-Western countries reluctant to rally to the West in isolating these countries, the international community in physical space is in some danger of fragmenting. This does not augur well for building an international community of states in cyberspace. The role of diplomats in both physical space and cyberspace will be crucial. Their aim, apart from keeping an international community of states together, should be the progressive integration of cyberspace and physical space. Rather than dealing with these areas separately, both diplomats and foreign ministries should treat them together, recognising the parallels in their structures and challenges.

Tackling cybersecurity and internet governance will require foreign ministries and diplomats to change.[10] Foreign ministries will need to be less hierarchical and more networked and will need to integrate diplomats posted abroad into the decision-making processes, while at the same time delegating more autonomy and authority to them. Cyber-space does not always allow time for consultation and hierarchical decision-making. Foreign ministries will also have to devote more thought to identifying and designing online platforms and digital tools to avoid the limitations imposed by social media. They need to develop exchanges with the tech industry to identify new technologies and how they will impact on international relations. Many will want to follow the example of the Danes and the French in appointing ambassadors to the tech industry, although as a result of the Facebook/Cambridge Analytica affair they will want to expand such ambassadors' remits to political issues. Diplomats will require training in new areas, includ-ing algorithms, search engine optimisation techniques and some levels of coding. But these are areas in which everyone will need training, and which new generations may learn at school together with reading and mathematics.

The greatest challenge for both foreign ministries and diplomats may be developing effective multi-stakeholder diplomacy for engaging with the full range of state and non-state actors. Firstly, diplomats will need to get better at identifying who the full range of non-state actors will be (including lower levels of government, such as cities). Secondly, foreign ministries must understand the stresses and difficulties of the same diplomats and diplomatic mis-sions dealing simultaneously with both state and non-state actors. This arose, for example, during the Arab Spring, when British diplomats in Egypt were expected to maintain normal relations with the Mubarak government while also analysing the intentions of the protesters. To the extent that they secured credibility with one side, they lost it with another (I have my own experience of this during the Tiananmen protests in Beijing, when discussing the future of Hong Kong with the Foreign Ministry in the morning and donning T-shirt and jeans in the afternoon to mix with the demonstrators). Above all, diplomats must recognise that not all non-state actors will want to talk to or collaborate with them. They will need to give thought to how they can use public diplomacy techniques (conferences, workshops, etc.) or surrogates to reach out to these more reluctant non-state actors so as to be able to engage with them in the debates.

Multi-stakeholder diplomacy is not the only area where twenty-first-century diplomats must be multifaceted, in both cyberspace and physical space. We have already discussed that they will need to deal with both cyberspace and physical space at the same time, integrating both domains with coherent foreign policies and diplomatic strategies. In both domains they will also have to consider simultaneously both the global issues and the geopolitical agendas (in cyberspace, the internet governance and cybersecurity agendas). They must not let the geopolitical agendas distract attention and effort from the global issues agendas, but nor must they allow their engagement in the global issues agendas to undermine their ability to respond firmly and effectively to geopolitical challenges. The difficulties of constructing some kind of order and stability in cyberspace reinforce the requirements of the transition to a multipolar system in physical space: to develop a hybrid statecraft combining the diplomatic approach with military and economic tools that incorporates both cyberspace and physical space, engages with multiple state and non-state actors, and manages global issues and geopolitical agendas. Diplomacy, as characterised by the diplomatic approach outlined in this book, is a necessary, if not sufficient, part of this statecraft.

Notes

Chapter 1 Introduction

1 Ben Farmer, Russia says Britain's defence secretary's claim of attack threat 'like something from Monty Python', *Daily Telegraph*, 26 January 2018, www.telegraph.co.uk/news/2018/01/25/crippling-russian-attack-britains-infrastructure-could-kill/.

2 Adam Segal, *The Hacked World Order: How Nations Fight, Trade, Maneuver, and Manipulate in the Digital Age* (New York: Public Affairs, 2017).

3 David E. Sanger, *Confront and Conceal: Obama's Secret Wars and Surprising Use of American Power* (New York: Broadway Paperbacks, 2012).

4 David E. Sanger: *The Perfect Weapon: War, Sabotage, and Fear in the Cyber Age* (New York: Crown, 2018).

5 Mark Mazzetti and Katie Benner, 12 Russian agents indicted in Mueller investigation, *New York Times*, 13 July 2018, www.nytimes.com/2018/07/13/us/politics/mueller-indictment-russian-intelligence-hacking.html.

6 Alexander Klimburg, *The Darkening Web: The War for Cyberspace* (New York: Penguin, 2017).

7 Jovan Kurbalija, *A Tipping Point for the Internet: Predictions for 2018* (Geneva: DiploFoundation, 2018).

8 Shaun Riordan, Cyberdiplomacy vs digital diplomacy: a terminological distinction, USC CPD blog, 12 May 2016, http://uscpublicdiplomacy.org/blog/cyber-diplomacy-vs-digital-diplomacy-terminological-distinction.

9 Corneliu Bjola and Marcus Holmes (eds), *Digital Diplomacy: Theory and Practice* (Abingdon: Routledge, 2015).

10 André Barrinha and Thomas Renard, Cyber-diplomacy: the making of an international society in the digital age, *Global Affairs*, 3 (2017): 353–64.

11 Shaun Riordan, *The Strategic Use of Digital and Public Diplomacy in Pursuit of National Objectives* (Barcelona: FOCIR, 2016), http://focir.cat/wp-content/uploads/2016/04/FOCIR_Pensament_1_Shaun-Riordan_Digital_Diplomacy1.pdf.

12 Carole Cadwalladr, How to bump Holocaust deniers off Google's top spot? Pay Google, *The Guardian*, 17 December 2016, www.theguardian.com/technology/2016/dec/17/holocaust-deniers-google-search-top-spot.

13 Shaun Riordan, The new international security agenda and the practice of diplomacy, in Andrew Cooper, Brian Hocking and William Maley (eds), *Global Governance and Diplomacy: Worlds Apart?* (Basingstoke: Palgrave Macmillan, 2008).

14 Robert D. Kaplan, *The Return of Marco Polo's World: War, Strategy, and American Interests in the Twenty-First Century* (New York: Random House, 2018).

Chapter 2 The Diplomat in Cyberspace

1 Jonathan Steinberg, *Bismarck: A Life* (Oxford: Oxford University Press, 2011).

2 Katharina Hone, Would the real diplomacy please stand up!, DiploFoundation blog, 30 June 2017, www.diplomacy.edu/blog/would-real-diplomacy-please-stand.

3 James M. Small, Business diplomacy in practice: advancing interests in crisis situations, *Hague Journal of Diplomacy*, 9/4 (2014): 374–92.

4 Paul Sharp, *Diplomatic Theory of International Relations* (Cambridge: Cambridge University Press, 2009).

5 Hedley Bull, *The Anarchical Society* (Basingstoke: Palgrave Macmillan, 1977).

6 Ludwig Wittgenstein, *Philosophical Investigations* (Oxford: Blackwell, 1978).
7 Barry Buzan, *An Introduction to the English School of International Relations* (Cambridge: Polity, 2014).
8 Paul Sharp, Revolutionary states, outlaw regimes and the techniques of public diplomacy, in Jan Melissen (ed.), *The New Public Diplomacy: Soft Power in International Relations* (Basingstoke: Palgrave Macmillan, 2005).
9 Gabriel Gorodetsky (ed.), *The Maisky Diaries: Red Ambassador to the Court of St James's, 1932–1943* (New Haven, CT: Yale University Press, 2015).
10 Alexander Klimburg, *The Darkening Web: The War for Cyberspace* (New York: Penguin, 2017).

Chapter 3　Regulating Cyberspace

1 Alexander Klimburg, *The Darkening Web: The War for Cyberspace* (New York: Penguin, 2017).
2 Ibid.
3 Ibid.
4 Ibid.
5 Jovan Kurbalija, *A Tipping Point for the Internet: Predictions for 2018* (Geneva: DiploFoundation, 2018).
6 Ibid.
7 Adam Segal, *The Hacked World Order: How Nations Fight, Trade, Maneuver, and Manipulate in the Digital Age* (New York: Public Affairs, 2017).
8 The Cambridge Analytica files, *The Guardian*, 11 July 2018, www.theguardian.com/news/series/cambridge-analytica-files.
9 EU GDPR portal, www.eugdpr.org/.
10 United States Department of Justice, Foreign Corrupt Practices Act, www.justice.gov/criminal-fraud/foreign-corrupt-practices-act.
11 David E. Sanger, *The Perfect Weapon: War, Sabotage, and Fear in the Cyber Age* (New York: Crown, 2018).
12 Kurbalija, *A Tipping Point for the Internet*.
13 Segal, *The Hacked World Order*.
14 Kurbalija, *A Tipping Point for the Internet*.

15 Jorge Pérez Martínez and Zoraida Frías Barroso, *Las Reglas del juego en el ecosistema digital – Level Playing Field* (Madrid: Fundación Telefónica, 2016).
16 Kurbalija, *A Tipping Point for the Internet*.
17 Rachel Botsman, Big Data meets Big Brother as China moves to rate its citizens, *Wired*, 21 October 2017, www.wired.co.uk/article/chinese-government-social-credit-score-privacy-invasion.
18 Don Tapscott and Alex Tapscott, *Blockchain Revolution: How the Technology Behind Bitcoin is Changing Money, Business and the World* (New York: Portfolio, 2016).

Chapter 4 Mitigating Cyberconflict

1 Alexander Klimburg, *The Darkening Web: The War for Cyberspace* (New York: Penguin, 2017).
2 David E. Sanger, *Confront and Conceal: Obama's Secret Wars and Surprising Use of American Power* (New York: Broadway Paperbacks, 2012).
3 Adam Segal, *The Hacked World Order: How Nations Fight, Trade, Maneuver, and Manipulate in the Digital Age* (New York: Public Affairs, 2017).
4 Florian Egloff, Cybersecurity and the age of privateering, in George Perkovich and Ariel E Levite (eds,) *Understanding Cyber Conflict: 14 Analogies* (Washington, DC: Georgetown University Press, 2017).
5 Segal, *The Hacked World Order*.
6 Robert A. Pape, *Dying to Win: The Strategic Logic of Suicide Terrorism* (New York: Random House, 2005).
7 David Patrikarakos, *War in 140 Characters: How Social Media is Reshaping Conflict in the Twenty-First Century* (New York: Basic Books, 2017); Tricia Jenkins, What did Russian trolls want in 2016? A closer look at the Internet Research Agency's active measures, War on the Rocks, 22 May 2018, https://warontherocks.com/2018/05/what-did-russian-trolls-want-during-the-2016-election-a-closer-look-at-the-internet-research-agencys-active-measures/.
8 Klimburg, *The Darkening Web*.
9 Gudrun Persson, *The War of the Future: A Conceptual Framework and Practical Conclusions: Essays on Strategic*

Thought, Russian Studies, 03/17 (Rome: Nato Defense College, 2017).

10 Klimburg, *The Darkening Web*.

11 Gordon Corera, *Intercept: The Secret History of Computers and Spies* (London: Weidenfeld & Nicolson, 2016).

12 Ben Buchanan, *The Cybersecurity Dilemma: Hacking Trust and Fear between Nations* (London: Hurst, 2016).

13 Michael Warner, Intelligence in cyber – and cyber in intelligence, in Perkovich and Levite (eds), *Understanding Cyberconflict*.

14 Klimburg, *The Darkening Web*.

15 Garrett M. Graff, Inside the hunt for Russia's most notorious hacker, *Wired*, 21 March 2017, www.wired.com/2017/03/russian-hacker-spy-botnet/.

16 CNN Cyber Shockwave, www.youtube.com/watch?v=02_z0dA3FKg.

17 Klimburg, *The Darkening Web*.

18 Jovan Kurbalija, *A Tipping Point for the Internet: Predictions for 2018* (Geneva: DiploFoundation, 2018).

19 Martin C. Libicki, *Cyberspace in Peace and War* (Annapolis, MD: Naval Institute Press, 2016).

20 Ibid.

21 Ibid.

22 Marcus Holmes, *Face-to-Face Diplomacy: Social Neuroscience and International Relations* (Cambridge: Cambridge University Press, 2018).

23 Ilan Manor, How diplomats can combat digital propaganda, *Global Policy Opinion*, 27 June 2018, www.globalpolicyjournal.com/blog/27/06/2018/how-diplomats-can-combat-digital-propaganda.

Chapter 5 Business and Cyberdiplomacy

1 Jennifer Kesteleyn, Shaun Riordan and Huub Ruël, Introduction: business diplomacy, *Hague Journal of Diplomacy*, 9/4 (2014): 303–9.

2 Adam Segal, *The Hacked World Order: How Nations Fight, Trade, Maneuver, and Manipulate in the Digital Age* (New York: Public Affairs, 2017).

3 James Lewis, *The Economic Impact of Cybercrime – No Slowing Down* (Santa Clara, CA: McAfee/CSIS, 2018).
4 Ponemon Institute, *2017 Cost of Cybercrime Study*, www.accenture.com/t20171006T095146Z__w__/us-en/_acnmedia/PDF-62/Accenture-2017CostCybercrime-US-FINAL.pdf#zoom=50.
5 EU GDPR portal, www.eugdpr.org/.
6 Jorge Pérez Martínez and Zoraida Frías Barroso, *Las Reglas del juego en el ecosistema digital – Level Playing Field* (Madrid: Fundación Telefónica, 2016).
7 Wally Olins, *Trading Identities: Why Countries and Companies are Taking on Each Other's Roles* (London: Foreign Policy Centre, 1999).
8 Jovan Kurbalija, *A Tipping Point for the Internet: Predictions for 2018* (Geneva: DiploFoundation, 2018).
9 Segal, *The Hacked World Order*.
10 Kurbalija, *A Tipping Point for the Internet*.

Chapter 6 Algorithms and Internet Companies

1 Shaun Riordan, We need to talk about algorithms, 5 November 2017, www.shaunriordan.com/?p=544.
2 Barbara Rosen Jacobson, Katharina E. Höne and Jovan Kurbalija, *Data Diplomacy: Updating Diplomacy to the Big Data Era* (Geneva: DiploFoundation, 2018).
3 Cathy O'Neil, *Weapons of Math Destruction: How Big Data Increases Inequality and Threatens Democracy* (New York: Crown, 2016).
4 Nicholas Dunbar, *Inventing Money: The Story of Long-Term Capital Management and the Legends behind It* (New York: John Wiley, 2000).
5 Pablo Triana, *Lecturing Birds on Flying: Can Mathematical Theories Destroy the Financial Markets?* (New York: John Wiley, 2009).
6 The Cambridge Analytica files, *The Guardian*, 11 July 2018, www.theguardian.com/news/series/cambridge-analytica-files.

7 Elisa Shearer and Jeffrey Gottfried, News use across social media platforms 2017, Pew Research Center, 7 September 2017.

8 Carole Cadwalladr, How to bump Holocaust deniers off Google's top spot? Pay Google, *The Guardian*, 17 December 2016, www.theguardian.com/technology/2016/dec/17/holocaust-deniers-google-search-top-spot.

9 Shaun Riordan, The really dark side of Facebook, USC Center on Public Diplomacy blog, 23 April 2018, https://uscpublic-diplomacy.org/blog/really-dark-side-facebook.

10 David Patrikarakos, *War in 140 Characters: How Social Media is Reshaping Conflict in the Twenty-First Century* (New York: Basic Books, 2017).

11 Ilan Manor, How diplomats can combat digital propaganda, *Global Policy Opinion*, 27 June 2018, www.globalpolicy-journal.com/blog/27/06/2018/how-diplomats-can-combat-digital-propaganda.

12 Office of Denmark's Tech Ambassador: http://techamb.um.dk/.

Chapter 7 Conclusion

1 Shaun Riordan, *The New Diplomacy* (Cambridge: Polity, 2003).

2 Edison Lee and Timothy Chau, *Telecom Services: The Geopolitics of 5G and IoT* (New York: Jefferies Group, 2017).

3 Paul Scharre, *Army of None: Autonomous Weapons and the Future of War* (New York: W. W. Norton, 2018).

4 Ibid.

5 Barbara Rosen Jacobson, *Searching for Meaningful Human Control: The April 2018 Meeting on Lethal Autonomous Weapons Systems*, Policy Papers and Briefs – 10 (Geneva: DiploFoundation, 2018).

6 Marcus Holmes, *Face-to-Face Diplomacy: Social Neuroscience and International Relations* (Cambridge: Cambridge University Press, 2018).

7 Nicholas Wheeler, *Trusting Enemies: Interpersonal Relationships in International Conflicts* (Oxford: Oxford University Press, 2018).

8 Stanley McChrystal et al., *Team of Teams: New Rules of Engagement for a Complex World* (London: Penguin, 2015).
9 Holmes, *Face-to-Face Diplomacy*.
10 Brian Hocking et al., *Whither Foreign Ministries in a Post-Western World*, Clingendael Policy Brief no. 20 (The Hague: Clingendael, 2013).

Index